TØ116376

Cambridge Elements ≡

Elements in Publishing and Book Culture
edited by
Samantha Rayner
University College London
Rebecca Lyons
University of Bristol

YOUNG ADULT FANTASY FICTION

Conventions, Originality, Reproducibility

Kim Wilkins
University of Queensland

CAMBRIDGE
UNIVERSITY PRESS

CAMBRIDGE
UNIVERSITY PRESS

University Printing House, Cambridge CB2 8BS, United Kingdom

One Liberty Plaza, 20th Floor, New York, NY 10006, USA

477 Williamstown Road, Port Melbourne, VIC 3207, Australia

314–321, 3rd Floor, Plot 3, Splendor Forum, Jasola District Centre,
New Delhi – 110025, India

79 Anson Road, #06–04/06, Singapore 079906

Cambridge University Press is part of the University of Cambridge.

It furthers the University's mission by disseminating knowledge in the pursuit of
education, learning, and research at the highest international levels of excellence.

www.cambridge.org
Information on this title: www.cambridge.org/9781108445320
DOI: 10.1017/9781108551137

First published 2019

A catalogue record for this publication is available from the British Library.

ISBN 978-1-108-44532-0 Paperback
ISSN 2514-8524 (online)
ISSN 2514-8516 (print)

Young Adult Fantasy Fiction

Conventions, Originality, Reproducibility

Elements in Publishing and Book Culture

DOI: 10.1017/9781108551137

First published online: July 2019

Kim Wilkins

University of Queensland

Author for correspondence: Kim Wilkins, k.wilkins@uq.edu.au

ABSTRACT: Young adult fantasy (YAF) brings together two established genres – young adult fiction and fantasy fiction – and in so doing amplifies, energises, and leverages the textual, social, and industrial practices of the two genres: combining the fantastic with adolescent concerns; engaging passionate online fandoms; proliferating quickly into series and related works. By considering the texts alongside the way they are circulated and marketed, this Element aims to show that the YAF genre is a dynamic formation that takes shape and reshapes itself responsively in a continuing process over time.

KEYWORDS: fantasy fiction, young adult fiction, fan communities, transmedia storyworlds, genre

ISBNs: 9781108445320 (PB), 9781108551137 (OC)

ISSNs: 2514-8524 (online), 2514-8516 (print)

Contents

Introduction: Genre and Young Adult Fantasy

In the United States, the world's biggest book market, young adult fantasy (YAF) has performed consistently well for a number of consecutive years. In 2014, juvenile fantasy fiction increased its market share by 38 per cent, levelled out in 2015, then rose a further 17 per cent in 2016 to become the biggest-selling juvenile category. While adult fantasy and science fiction combined sold 11,856,000 units in 2016, the same combined category in juvenile fiction sold 52,255,000 units, or more than four times as many (Milliot, 2015, 2016, 2017).[1] This success extends beyond the US market. For example, according to Sarah J. Maas's website, her YAF series *Throne of Glass* has now been translated into thirty-five different languages, and Cassandra Clare's publisher Simon & Schuster boasts that she has 50 million copies of her books in print worldwide. These figures indicate a global dissemination and robust market power across the world. Young adult fantasy texts also serve as originating texts for transmedia adaptations, both official and non-official: from high-budget screen adaptations and licensed tie-in products to peer-to-peer merchandising and fan fiction. High-profile adaptations can lead to stardom for actors who take iconic roles (e.g., Emma Watson, Robert Pattinson), securely tying YAF to broader celebrity culture and mainstream media interest (Steveker, 2015: 148). In many ways, YAF's operations are emblematic of developments and disruptions in the publishing industry and reading practices of the twenty-first century, and yet our scholarly understanding of the genre's commercial, social, and creative operations is not rigorous or nuanced.

The new publishing paradigm's tendency towards franchising, convergence, reproducibility, and fan culture has been well served by a series of megaselling young adult fiction (YA) texts in the twenty-first century, such as the Harry Potter, Twilight, and *The Hunger Games* series. These

---

[1] Nielsen BookScan counts adult science fiction and fantasy separately, while juvenile science fiction/fantasy/magic is one category. I have combined the adult categories to make the comparison more accurate, but see later in this Element for definitions of how this Element understands fantasy. Note that the juvenile category also includes children's fiction, but the scale of comparison is still dramatic.

successes and others like them inspire acquisition of books that might function similarly in the marketplace, to both satisfy and stimulate audience need. Publishers and booksellers often frame new acquisitions in relation to existing texts. When HarperTeen acquired Victoria Aveyard's debut YAF series *Red Queen* in a 'major' deal ('major' being a trade euphemism for a deal worth more than US$500,000), the book was described in *Publishers Marketplace* as '*Graceling* meets *The Selection*' (2013). Kiera Cass's *The Selection* itself was initially pitched as '*The Hunger Games* meets *The Bachelor*' (2010), while Kristin Cashore's influential YAF *Graceling* has 'met' many other sources over the past ten years (including *Swan Lake*, *Pride and Prejudice*, and *The Mists of Avalon*). In 2016–17, Aveyard's *Red Queen* was a common reference text on *Publishers Marketplace*, 'meeting' *Girl on the Train* (Astrid Scholte's *Four Dead Queens*), *Downton Abbey* (Sara Holland's *The Everless Girl*), and *East of Eden* (Joelle Charbonneay's *Dividing Eden*), all in 'significant' six-figure deals. This so-called X-meets-Y formulation for describing texts is common enough to warrant an entry on fandom wiki *tvtropes*, complete with a 'pitch generator' that throws up random pairings such as 'Maze Runner meets The Divine Comedy' (tvtropes 'Just for Fun'). Its almost risible commonness, however, underscores how crucial it remains for the industry to triangulate the location of texts among similar texts, or to support the production of what Corbett calls 'read-alikes' (2014: np). The size of the advances in the cases noted earlier points to a high level of confidence in the read-alike's potential for success.

These X-meets-Y constructions describe texts, that is, they suggest their textual features: Cassandra Clare's *The Mortal Instruments* series is sometimes pitched as *Harry Potter* meets *Twilight*, because the story is about a young woman who discovers she has magical abilities *and* deals with a complicated paranormal romance. But the industry does not simply use X meets Y to describe the texts; it also clearly uses the construction to predict what the text *will do* among readers and in the publishing industry, including how it might circulate and sell, and which existing routes to market it might exploit. When we talk about fiction publishing, it has become 'second nature' to understand the market in terms of genre (Berberich, 2015: 30), and the X-meets-Y formulation is strongly evocative of the reproducibility and comparability with which conceptualisations of genre are so often associated. How, then, might genre provide a useful insight into the twenty-first-century publishing phenomenon of YAF?

Genre encompasses so much more than the content of texts, and a genre perspective may shift arguments away from description and definition, and towards an understanding of the processes that constitute relationships between authors, readers, and the institutions that bring them together (Wilkins, 2005: np). Genres are not static and unchanging categories that can be defined checklist style (the notorious 'formula' by which the popular press often judges genre fiction). Rather, they are dynamic formations that respond and circulate socially and industrially, forming and reforming over time. Approaching the study of any genre would imply an analysis of not only the texts, but also potentially its audience, its marketing, its book design, its paratexts, and so on, because these are all part of the complex process by which the genre is formed. This Element frames the discussion of YAF in terms of this broader definition of genre to achieve two aims. The first aim is to produce a short but multifaceted study of a largely untheorised field of literature that has great cultural reach. This Element shows the way that YAF brings together two established genres with devoted readerships – young adult fiction and fantasy fiction – and in so doing amplifies and energises some of the most recognisable aspects of these two genres: that is, it seeks to unpack some of the specific processes of the X-meets-Y formulation. The second aim is to demonstrate how an examination of a popular genre might look, if it paid attention to the multiple dimensionality of genre – its textual, social, and industrial operations – and the links between them. This Element is intended as a model of a sophisticated and productive reading of one of the most popular of the popular genres, making room for understanding YAF's textual conventions alongside the way it is circulated and enjoyed.

Defining Young Adult Fantasy

The definition of 'fantasy fiction' is now a creaking superstructure on top of the genre, and does not seem to be able to move far from taxonomy. In part, this concern with pinning down a definition arises from the necessity for key concepts to analyse. Attebery gets around this cul-de-sac with his emphasis on 'fuzzy sets' that are defined 'not by boundaries but by a centre' (1992: 12), and this is perhaps the most useful way of approaching taxonomy. But what is at the centre of fantasy's 'fuzzy set'? Clute emphasises 'perceived impossibility', but then becomes a little more prescriptive about structure: 'A fantasy text may be described as the story of an earned passage from Bondage – via a central Recognition of what has been revealed and of what is about to happen, and which may involve a profound Metamorphosis of protagonist or world (or both) – into the Eucatastrophe, where marriages may occur, just governance fertilises the barren Land, and there is a Healing' (1997: np). Mendlesohn eschews conventions and structures, and places her emphasis on rhetoric. She sees fantasy as a 'fiction of consensual construction of belief', which relies on 'literary techniques . . . most appropriate to the reader expectations' gesturing to the reader's role in constructing the genre (2008: xi), and distinguishes five subcategories of fantasy that have specific 'stylistic needs' (xv). These field-defining works have performed important literary analysis and have opened up influential perspectives from which the academy can talk about fantasy, and in doing so have legitimated discussion of a genre often dismissed as trivial or even childish. But framing fantasy fiction from a purely literary perspective may play into the constrained definitions that see genre as reducible solely to what is observable *within* the texts. Such definitions, because they describe static content, are often used to underscore the genre's alleged formulaic nature and to suggest its limits, rather than recognising the wider social and industrial processes that traverse and shape genre texts.

Rather than striving for a more complicated or precise definition of the fantasy genre that adds key terms to the field of study, I adhere to a 'we know it when we see it' approach to fantasy fiction, using the collective pronoun 'we' to reference all of those who have a view on the genre. Those who are invested – writers, readers, publishers, and even academics – can recognise fantasy without a checklist: it is written like fantasy, it is packaged like fantasy, it circulates like fantasy, and it reads like fantasy from the perspective of those writing it, packaging it, circulating it, and reading it. As an example, Kazuo Ishiguro's novel *The Buried Giant* inspired a vigorous debate in literary pages, which included opinions from Neil Gaiman and Ursula K. Le Guin, about whether or not it was a fantasy novel. The text featured many of the common conventions of fantasy, including dragons, medievalism, a quest narrative, and so on. But the text did not substantially operate as fantasy on a social or industrial level. The flurry of opinions that this text aroused about genre saw genre too narrowly defined by textual features only. The texts that are the focus of this Element are written by writers who are also readers of fantasy, are supported by paratexts such as jacket design and internal map illustrations that actively mark them as fantasy, are stocked in specialist fantasy bookstores, and are discussed on *Goodreads* as fantasy by readers. There is no mistaking what they are.

I have deliberately chosen not to use the term 'speculative fiction' in this Element, as it is not a meaningful term in an industry sense. In the United States, the Book Industry Studies Group's BISAC Subject Codes do not include speculative fiction, offering instead fifteen subcategories of fantasy. Nielsen BookScan also has no speculative fiction category. Thema, the international book trade's categorisation scheme, does list speculative fiction, but it is an unelaborated category, unlike the nine different fantasy categories. Importantly, science fiction does not fall within this Element's scope; the fantastic powers in all the texts under discussion are attributable to magic or the supernatural, not to science or technology. This Element is interested in a variety of subcategories of fantasy: first, the highly recognisable 'high' or 'epic' fantasy, set in secondary worlds where magic exists, for example, Sarah J. Maas's *Throne of Glass* series or Kristin Cashore's *Graceling* and its companion texts; second, the horror-adjacent 'low' or 'urban' fantasy, where mythological creatures interact with the real world, for example, Cassandra Clare's *The Mortal Instruments* series or Maggie Stiefvater's *Raven Cycle*; and third, the post–*The Hunger Games* dystopic fantasy, where cinematic-style superpowers are put into play in crushingly oppressive worlds, such as Victoria Aveyard's *Red Queen* series, or Marie Lu's *Young Elites* series.

The definition of 'young adult fiction' (YA) seems as though it should be more straightforward; the term itself suggests that the expected audience guides the definition and that these are books written for teenagers. To a certain extent this is true. However, YA is a 'mixed market' (Spencer, 2017: 433). Many adults read it (though estimations of the size of that proportion of readers differ), and most texts are 'written by adults, published by adults, reviewed by adults as well as marketed by and, in fact, for adults as they are usually the ones who make books available to children both educationally and economically' (Steveker, 2015: 150). While YA is often classed as a subset of children's literature, it also has a liminal character, disrupting 'the binary opposition between adult and child' (Phillips, 2015: 45). Young adult fiction certainly features central adolescent characters and situations adolescents might be concerned with – interacting with adult characters and institutions, understanding and solidifying their identities, forming relationships, both cooperative and adversarial, with other young adults – but it hails an audience much wider than adolescents, offering pleasure to much younger readers (who may, perhaps, enjoy it aspirationally) and to much older readers (who may, perhaps, enjoy it nostalgically).

Again, I apply the 'we know it when we see it' principle to defining YA. Young adult fiction texts are clearly designed and circulated as different from adult books in a range of ways. First, the page extent of the books is generally, though by no means always, shorter than that of most adult books excluding literary fiction and category romance, and the font is sometimes larger. These aspects of the text indicate the word length is shorter and, by extension, the plot less likely to be complicated by subplots and proliferating viewpoint characters. Second, young adult books also regularly sell at a different price point from adult books. For example, the Australian recommended retail price (RRP) for Robin Hobb's May 2017 trade paperback of her adult fantasy *Assassin's Fate* is AU$32.99, compared to Cassandra Clare's YAF *Lord of Shadows* at AU$27.99 for the same format and publication month (www.booktopia.com). Third, distribution methods differ. While YA is sold in trade in high volume, these books also form a large portion of standing orders for libraries and educational institutions. It is perhaps for this reason that much scholarship about YA fiction frames it in terms of its community or educational value. For example, Kaplan's review of research into the genre is concerned almost solely with literacy education and the perennial question of whether or not 'kids are reading' (2011: 72). But as Richards points out, the educational imperative of YA fiction is not the whole story at all; rather, YA has the potential to meet a wide, commercial audience (2007: 153). Richards's point, considered more than ten years after publication, almost bears the character of understatement.

Perhaps most significantly, though, YA is recognisable as YA because its narratives are focalised overwhelmingly through teenage protagonists.

Following from these definitions, then, the texts I have chosen to make central to this study feature young adult characters engaged in stories where magic or the supernatural is a significant part of the plot logic. This Element focusses on the twenty-first century, a period of pervasive change in the way books are acquired, published, and circulated. Notwithstanding the popularity of books by J. R. R. Tolkien and George R. R. Martin, which have been given a sizeable boost by recent televisual adaptations, YAF is the dominant expression of fantasy fiction in this century. At the time of writing, a ten-year anniversary edition of Cassandra Clare's *City of Bones* was in press. This seems an ideal point from which to examine the cultural phenomenon of YAF.

Applying the logic that the cultural reach of this genre is one of the most interesting things about it, I selected texts based on their popularity. I canvassed readers on forums and social media; I combed through *Goodreads* entries to find the most reviewed YAF books; but most importantly, I decided by the level of 'ambient noise' about the books and their authors. For example, I noted anecdotes about huge crowd-drawing potential at writers' festivals and conventions, deal news in trade publications, books teenagers were reading on the train, window displays in bookstores, attention paid to certain authors on reading and writing forums. In some sense, the three case studies found me – a bookish fantasy reader open to YA – and I have allowed that natural market penetration to guide my choices. Applying these controls, it soon became clear that the study would be dominated by white, female authors from North America. Rather than add a token author from the United Kingdom or my home publishing environment of Australia, I have decided to let my selections stand: this is what YAF looked like at the time of writing. I read through a wide selection of texts and narrowed it down to those that would yield the most compelling evidence for my arguments, sticking largely with single texts to suit the scope of this short monograph, although all chosen texts are published in series. The texts I consider are Sarah J. Maas's *Throne of Glass*, Cassandra Clare's *City of Bones*, and Victoria Aveyard's *Red Queen*. This Element describes and analyses the very recent history of YAF, not only by reading the texts, but also by situating those texts within their contexts. Textual analysis is valuable scholarship, but on its own will not deepen understanding of a genre. Genre is formed in the complex interrelations between text, audience, and industry; this Element seeks to understand that process by paying due attention across all three.

Conceptualising Genre

The word 'genre' comes to us, via French, from the Latin *genus*, which means family or kind. Family resemblances among popular genres continue to arouse disdain from some sectors, because resemblance is not valued in a still highly Romanticised literary sphere: indeed, resemblance is equated with the derivative and unoriginal. While John Frow's 2007 text on genre does not directly focus on popular genres of fiction, his conceptualisations are nonetheless applicable. He suggests that useful contemporary theory on genre is lacking because of the 'the continuing of a neoclassical understanding of genre as prescriptive taxonomy and as a constraint on textual energy' and so accounts of genre are subject to 'Romantic reaction' (2007: 1627).

While a more widespread understanding and acceptance of genre fiction has developed since the turn of the twenty-first century, it is still far from uncommon to find scholars who see popular genres of fiction as 'written to a strict formula that unintentionally stifles the writer's creativity and leads to dry, unreadable prose' (Faktorovich, 2014: 2). Faktorovich goes on to use the word 'hack' as her key term to describe writers of popular fiction (6), and opines that they write to a 'set of established formulas that have been designed by marketers, publishers, and profit-minded authors' (1). Fred Botting agrees, suggesting the 'formulaic and mechanical set of conventions' (2012: 159) are part of the 'straightforwardly commercial' aims of popular fiction (163). He goes one step further though, associating these commercial aims with the ideological goal (whose, he does not say) of 'reinforcing prevailing attitudes and assumptions, reassuring existing norms and values to the point of indoctrination' (163). This (alarmingly) recent scholarship tells us there is still a great deal of misunderstanding about how genres operate in the field of popular fiction and in the wider fields of creativity and publishing studies. It is clear that a more lucid and nuanced conceptualisation of genre is needed, one that can respond to the inter-related complexities of textual, social, and industrial processes of genre formation and yield new insights into book culture.

Despite Faktorovich's and Botting's assumption that narrow sets of textual conventions are the chief markers of genre, the idea that genres are more fluid and more negotiated than that has a solid history. Tzvetan Todorov, one of the earliest theorists of the fantastic mode, rejects the idea that genres are fixed, ahistorical categories. Any text can be seen as a 'product' of an existing 'combinatorial system' but importantly it is also 'a transformation of that system' (1973: 7). Each genre is structured by its own regimes of verisimilitude, which are consistent with what is commonly believed to belong to that genre at that time. Verisimilitude as a concept only makes sense when we decentre the text as the sole determiner of genre. Genre, for Todorov, exists in a relationship between the text and the reader. Likewise, Hans Robert Jauss is interested in interactions between texts and readers in the formation of genres. In particular, his concept of a 'horizon of expectations' is useful for describing the way that genres operate. For Jauss, expectations guide readings. The image of the 'horizon' suggests those expectations surround readers but are not fixed. As readers move, so do horizons. This implied movement means that a new text can evoke 'the horizon of expectations and "rules of the game" extended, corrected, but also transformed, crossed out, or simply reproduced' (1982: 88). Jauss recognises here not only that genres change over time, but also that audiences are involved in shaping those changes. For Jonathan Culler, just as we all approach communication armed with a competence formed of 'implicit knowledge' and 'internalised grammar,' so do we also approach literary works with a literary competence. Literary works, he writes, 'have structure and meaning because [they] are read in a particular way' (1975: 113). Literary competence describes the reader's ability to comprehend a text in particular contexts that have been learned through reading. We might say genre competence is the reader's ability to comprehend (and appreciate) a genre text through a lifetime of interaction with that genre.

The idea that genres are negotiated between texts and readers has been elaborated in more recent scholarship. Brian McHale references the idea, writing of 'shared conventions' and genre fiction's proclivity to 'cater more openly to the expectations of readers familiar with these conventions' (2010: np), while Peter Dixon and Marisa Bortolussi write that 'genre can be understood as an implicit contract between readers and the producers of commercial narratives and that this contract is mediated by readers' knowledge', which is shaped by 'reading experience' (2009: 542–3). They also point out that genre distinctions are caught up 'in many aspects of marketing and publishing' (2009: 542), thus gesturing to the industrial aspects of genre formation. This third aspect of genre formation, the industrial, adds an extra dimension for study. Jauss, with his interest in the material specificity of genre formation, has already made room for structures other than the social to be implicated. Frow also argues for a 'poetics in which the structural components of genre are taken to be historically specific' (2007: 1628), and historical specificity might include understanding conditions of production and circulation. Frow rightly points to film theory as a 'potential source of [genre theory's] renewal' (1629). The fields of film and television studies have always been more comfortable with genre than has literary studies. Differences in production and circulation notwithstanding, there is much we might borrow in understanding popular genres of fiction from theory about popular genres of film and television, especially at a time when book culture is so caught up in transmedia convergence. Film theorist Steve Neale, for example, argues that the relationship between text and audience is highly mediated through industry and other institutions (1995: 162–3). Studying genres across creative, audience, and institutional perspectives, as Jason Mittell argues about television genres, allows for a shift in focus to 'a circuit of cultural practice operative in multiple sites, instead of a singular realm of textual criticism or institutional analysis' (2004: ix). A wider perspective of genre opens up the possibility of showing the various interrelated sites of cultural agency that are activated by YAF texts.

Dixon and Bortolussi grasp this conceptualisation of genre in one sense: they write that 'readers have certain expectations concerning the nature of works in a given genre, and authors and publishers contrive to fulfil those expectations' by 'adapt[ing] their products accordingly' (2009: 544–5). But in another sense, they miss something crucial about the negotiations between writers, readers, and industry, in that those negotiations are invested, sometimes passionate, often pleasurable. The model

Dixon and Bortolussi imagine operates in one direction: the producers of genre 'doing' genre at readers. In fact, genre is far more dynamic, responsive, and agential. On the one hand, the market is large and diverse, and 'the sheer number of individual product lines calls out for some sort of taxonomy' so that texts and readers can find each other: marketing is central to that 'taxonomic enterprise' (Squires, 2007: 71). On the other hand, though, genres create markets. They have 'as much ... agency in the publishing field as publishers, booksellers and the other symbolic brokers ... Writers and readers are located within the communication circuits of book production and knowledge transmission both in accordance with and reaction against dominant genres' (72). Genre, then, is a dynamic access point for understanding how texts work in the world.

In previous scholarship, Lisa Fletcher, Beth Driscoll, and I developed the concept of a 'genre world', borrowing from Howard Becker's 'art world', to describe 'the collective activity that goes into the creation and circulation of genre texts', with a particular focus on social and industrial uses of texts. This concept expands the study of popular fiction beyond an overemphasis on the 'textual dimensions of genre' – which often leads to decisionist readings that rate the ideological value of texts – into a 'broader view' that contextualises the variety of cultural work that genres such as YAF perform (Fletcher, Driscoll, and Wilkins, 2018: 998–1000). This tripartite methodology for the study of a particular genre like YAF would reveal not only how YAF texts are defined, but also how they are enjoyed, published, and circulated. This Element models such a methodology in order to understand better the cultural operations of YAF: textually, socially, and industrially. When X meets Y, not only are expectations set, but new energy potentially arises that both shapes and responds to specific cultural moments across the various sectors of book culture. 'Fantasy meets YA' is one of the twenty-first century's most visible and successful meetings.

Section Outlines

The textual, social, and industrial aspects of genre are not easily separable from each other, and that becomes clear throughout this Element. Genre tropes spill out of books and into social discussions; social discussions pressure publishers to change the contents of books; and market success influences the choices writers make about how to use or combine genre elements. Nonetheless, each section that follows centralises a key aspect of genre formation.

Section 1 considers the YAF genre as a *textual* formation. It seeks a new perspective on the most recognisable textual conventions associated with fantasy: the high fantasy tropes of a cruel past, a series of tests, and a Chosen One. These tropes, reproduced to the point of parody in late twentieth-century fantasy in the wake of Tolkien's *The Lord of the Rings*, have been subtly repurposed for a twenty-first-century audience, becoming merged with YA conventions. Using Sarah J. Maas's *Throne of Glass*, this section considers the way genres respond over time to changing audience and industry expectations. How does the cruel past present a potentially oppressive context for adolescent characters? How do fantasy tests and trials become adolescent battlegrounds? And how does the Chosen One speak to ideas about teenage identity?

In Section 2, my focus turns to the *social* formation of genre, in particular to considering the ways that the notion of originality is defined and debated among YAF readers and reviewers over Cassandra Clare's *The Mortal Instruments* series. I start with a close reading of how creative expression is represented in the text, then widen to how the same ideas are worked out in the enthusiastically engaged interactions of fantasy fandom, how fans use existing texts, and how debates are amplified by an adolescent, (assumed) digitally native audience. Drawing on fan forums, *Goodreads*, and media reports, I explore how the concept of originality becomes troubled by Clare's background as a writer of Harry Potter fan fiction. Debates about ethical practice in fandom follow: what it is allowable to repeat (and how), what draws judgement, and who makes those decisions. The section also considers the social institution of the law, and the legal case brought by Sherrilyn Kenyon on Cassandra Clare over copyright infringement. Fandom's 'rules' and 'policing' are compared with actual legal institutions and how they deal with genre.

Section 3 turns to the idea of reproducibility, or how success in YAF is intentionally reproduced in an *industrial* sense, using Victoria Aveyard's *Red Queen* as the key text and drawing from industry reports and academic theories of convergence and transmedia storytelling. The proliferative character of the fantasy genre is explored, in terms of how settings and situations extend beyond individual books into maps, glossaries, guidebooks, and digital assets. The importance of the series is considered, particularly how repeated tropes are related to repeated sales, and how acquisition and marketing are related to taste-making in the field. Finally, I consider convergence across media, how a series becomes a franchise, and the importance of licensing, adaptation, and transmedia storytelling.

This Element, then, considers YAF as a genre, and in so doing seeks to expand the boundaries of how we conceptualise genre and to offer new ways of thinking through the interrelated investments of book culture in the twenty-first century.

1 Conventions and the Text

Something evil dwells in this castle, something wicked enough to make the stars quake. Its malice echoes into all worlds . . . Erilea needs you as the King's Champion. (Maas, 2012: 186)

The opening quotation of this section, spoken by the ghostly Queen Elena to hero Celaena Sardothien in Sarah J. Maas's *Throne of Glass*, could not be mistaken for any other genre than fantasy. Castles, dualistic good and evil, fantastic realms, and an unlikely saviour are such common tropes that they are sometimes derided as cliché, or parodied affectionately by fantasy readers: see, for example, Diana Wynne-Jones's 1996 *Tough Guide to Fantasyland*. Nonetheless, the tropes persist, particularly in the most recognisable subgenre of fantasy, high or epic fantasy. This subgenre remains highly visible in the twenty-first century due to film adaptations of popular fiction texts and the mainstreaming of fantasy role-playing video games such as *World of Warcraft* and *Skyrim*, and their continued success in the marketplace indicates continuing pleasure is available to audiences engaging with them. These high fantasy conventions derive largely from the post-Tolkien fantasy of the late twentieth century – for example, Terry Brooks's *Shannara* series or Robert Jordan's *Wheel of Time* series – but have endured over time.

Jauss advocates for genres to be read diachronically. He argues that reading takes place within a historically specific situation, so the horizon of expectation for any genre is specific to 'the historical moment of its appearance, from a previous understanding of the genre, from the form and themes of already familiar works' (1970: 11). Rather than seeing high fantasy conventions as static markers of the genre, this section sees them as dynamic and historically specific intervention points for the adjacent genre of YA to engage with. That is, if classic fantasy tropes are 'X', then how do the YA conventions of 'Y' exploit or expand on them? This question has a particularly twenty-first-century complexion. Certainly, fantasy for young adults is not new: the works of Alan Garner or Ursula K. Le Guin come immediately to mind. However, recent book history is dominated by YA megasellers with a market penetration that goes far beyond anything Garner or Le Guin could have imagined, writing as they were in a vastly different publishing paradigm.

Young adult fantasy texts such as Sarah J. Maas's *Throne of Glass*, Sabaa Tahir's *An Ember in the Ashes*, or Kristin Cashore's *Graceling* reuse classic high fantasy conventions such as pre-modern settings, series of trials, and unlikely heroes. But, as Neale writes of film genres, in texts, conventions are not only replayed, but also 'in play' (1995: 170–1). This section demonstrates the value of close textual analysis in understanding genre, by analysing the way fantasy conventions, specifically long-standing high fantasy conventions, can be used for YA purposes in YAF.

The Cruel Past

In *Throne of Glass*, Celaena Sardothien (also known, in later books, as Aelin Galathynius) is a teenage assassin, feared across the land of Erilea. Orphaned as a child, she was rescued from the streets and then trained by a famous assassin and cruel father figure, Arobynn Hamel. Her record as a killer sees her imprisoned in the salt mines of Endovier, where, after a year of brutal treatment, she frees herself for long enough to kill dozens of guards before violent recapture. When the king of Adarlan's captain, Chaol Westfall, arrives to speak to her, she believes she will face the death penalty. However, he tells her she can choose instead to go to Rifthold to compete for the role of King's Assassin. Savage and wily, Celaena agrees and is installed in the king's glass castle, where she trains for the competition; she also tries on dresses, learns the manners of the court, and becomes beloved both of Chaol and Prince Dorian. As Celaena reflects on the deal she has made, she is increasingly uncomfortable in the knowledge that being the King's Assassin means serving a social system that has oppressed her and those she has loved. Moreover, in the castle are secret passageways, killer demons, and the ghost of a dead elven queen who seems to know more about Celaena than she knows about herself.

Our common imaginings of the pre-modern are embedded in almost every aspect of this brief plot summary: from the spelling (the 'ae' combination of medieval languages), to the oppressive regime (slaves, salt mines, feudal social structures), to the fairy tale castle with its potential for Cinderella-like transformation and romance (Maas has noted that Cinderella was a significant influence on the creation of the text), to the supernatural beasts and prophecies in the castle's hidden rooms and passages. The setting of the story borrows from a range of historical periods to create a generalised sense of the past, but it is a past that has a cruel inflection. *Red Queen* author Victoria Aveyard has told how her own cruel past setting is inspired by the Roman Empire (as is the work of Sabaa Tahir) because she wanted to 'play with a modern Dark Ages' (in Baver, 2015: np). This quotation troubles any attempt to hold the borders of periodisation (classical, medieval, modern), revealing the use of historical settings as having less to do with accuracy than with the potential for enriching a narrative. As Stephanie Trigg notes, 'the demands of art [or in this case genre] will always trump the demands of history' (2008: 100).

Fantasy fiction's embedded use of pre-industrial medieval settings is readily apparent, and most visible in the epic or high fantasy iterations of the genre. From J. R. R. Tolkien, who drew on his scholarly background in medieval literature for his *The Lord of the Rings* series, to George R. R. Martin, who popularised the so-called gritty Middle Ages in his *A Song of Ice and Fire* series, the genre has used and reused the settings, mythology, history, and culture of the past endemically. Sarah J. Maas, who calls herself a 'hardcore fan' of Tolkien (Yang, 2016: np), continues in this tradition, as we can see in this description of the medievalist city Rifthold, early in *Throne of Glass*:

> Trumpeters signalled their arrival as they passed through
> the looming alabaster walls of Rifthold. Crimson flags
> depicting gold wyverns flapped in the wind above the capital
> city, the cobblestone streets were cleared of traffic, and
> Celaena . . . frowned as the odor of the city met her nose.
> (Maas, 2012: 39)

The epic scope of fantasy is enhanced by scenes such as these, which
emphasise height and size and bold colour. But the grittiness of contemporary medievalist fantasy is here too, with the 'ambient smelliness' of the
medieval world noted, referencing the common 'collocation of the pre-
modern with odour' that serves to distance the modern audience from the
cruel past (D'Arcens, 2011: 165–6). In this scene, which functions as an
'establishing shot' of one of the key settings of the book, Maas shows that
she can grasp and reproduce one of the staple elements of the genre, that of
the pre-modern city.

Louise Fradenburg sees representations of the Middle Ages as 'secur[ing],
for modernity, its intelligibility to itself' (1997: 211), which it does by
bracketing the pre-modern off in our cultural narrative of supercession and
imagining it as 'dense, unvarying, and eminently obvious monolith' against
which the enlightened modern (and knowing postmodern) emerges
(Dinshaw, 1999: 15–19). That is, we know that we are modern (and, I
would argue, Western) because our society is not irrational, floridly religious,
and normatively violent, at least not to the extent that society in the Middle
Ages is imagined to be. But the irrational, floridly religious, and normatively
violent exercise powers of attraction over us too, and nowhere is that more
clear than in fantasy fiction. Because the past is cruel – unsafe, non-
democratic, superstitious, often lawless, always violent – it provides a rich,
dramatic context within which characters can act. A large part of the pre-
modern's appeal in fantasy fiction, then, is in the way it enhances the narrative
interest of any story.

This dramatic potential of the cruel past is amplified in YA iterations of
fantasy, because in the pre-modern period, teenagers were not seen as in
need of parental guidance, but were 'genuinely occupied with adulthood'
(Levy and Mendlesohn, 2016: 210). Historical settings allow young adult

characters to drive the narrative with more agency, and to do so from a less safe social position, because they are not cocooned by family. In writerly parlance, the narrative stakes for teenage characters in pre-modern settings are very high indeed, with the end result of a more thrilling and fast-paced plot. The cruel past adds pressure to Celaena's choices and actions, increasing the urgency of the narrative. In the competition to become King's Champion, all of Celaena's fellow competitors are brutal and dangerous, including a man known as Scythe, 'for the weapon he'd used to torture and hack apart temple priestesses' (Maas, 2012: 87). Celaena is forced to obey under threat of violent public death: 'Any wrongdoing on your part, and I'll stake you to the front gates' (69). Runes called 'Wyrdmarks' are found at the site of a 'ritualistic' killing (195). The king's voice is described as 'edged with the clash of shields and the scream of arrows' (47), as though the oppressive patriarch's body and medieval violence are one and the same thing. The overwhelming impression is a setting where genuine danger is always at hand, because this society is not yet enlightened or modern.

This pre-modern past is particularly cruel to women. Jane Tolmie argues that fantasy fiction 'depends on ideas about medieval patriarchy to delineate exceptional women', representing the pre-modern world as a time of 'gender-based oppression' that can serve as a dramatic backdrop for a particular kind of 'exceptional' heroine (2006: 146). Pitching Celaena in a battle to the death against twenty-three male competitors can certainly be read as a fairly obvious metaphor for the kind of oppressive patriarchal context women faced in the cruel past. Celaena also has to contend with gender-based rules such as curtseying, which she thinks of as 'courtly nonsense' (Maas, 2012: 73); uncomfortably constricting dresses that make her long for men's clothes: '*This* was why she mostly preferred tunics and pants' (46); and sexual insults, for example, when one of the other champions suggests in training that she would be 'better off on your back, learning tricks useful to a woman' (107–8).

Key aspects of the plot show Celaena reversing expectations about her gender role in this acutely oppressive setting. For example, during an archery practice, she shoots more accurately than any of the men: 'The arrow hit the absolute centre [of the target], obliterating the black dot. They stopped laughing' (Maas, 2012: 118–19). The syntax in the short, pithy line acts almost as a full stop, demonstrating Celaena's ability to put an end to the criticisms of those who seek to oppress her because of her sex. Celaena, in many ways, exemplifies medievalist fantasy's exceptional woman. As Tolmie explains, the exceptionalism arises from her difference from other women: 'The 'independent, strong, feisty, and passionate' heroine 'does not exist within a system in which all women are independent, strong, feisty, and passionate . . . Behind her and all around her is the silent rank and file of women who do not choose, elude, or escape', that is 'the exception depends on the general condition' (2006: 146). Celaena proudly differentiates herself from other kinds of women: '"[W]hat's wrong with headstrong girls?"' she asks Chaol, '"Other than the fact that they're not wooden-headed ninnies who can only open their mouths to give orders and gossip?"' (Maas, 2012: 102). Here, Celaena imagines other women who do not resist the patriarchal system and who are overly concerned with trivial matters. Elsewhere, she casts suspicion more generally, having 'sworn never to trust girls again' after all her previous friends have 'disappointed her' (101). Her female nemesis in the glass castle is Lady Kaltain Rompier, whose name, reminiscent of the childish or playfully sexual 'romping', suggests a lack of serious agency. Kaltain is painfully envious of Celaena – whom she thinks of as a 'conniving harlot whore' (298) – largely because of the sexual interest Celaena arouses in many of the most powerful and desirable men in the glass castle. This envy means Kaltain readily becomes the pawn of Duke Perrington. Perrington plots to kill Celaena by poison before the last tournament, a suggestion that makes Kaltain more breathless than her 'too-tight corset' (306).

> Perrington grasped her hands. His ring was ice-cold against her skin, and she fought the urge to rip her hands from his grip. 'Don't you want to help Dorian? Once he's free of her . . .' *Then he'll be mine. He'll be mine as he should be.* (307)

When Kaltain is dangerous, she is not agentially and violently dangerous like Celaena: indeed, she cannot even bring herself to resist Perrington's grasp (or a corset that is too tight). Rather, she willingly assists a man to commit a murder by stealth, inspired by trivial sexual jealousy. These aspects of Kaltain's behaviour – her lack of agency and her fixation on romantic rivalry – are reminiscent of the kind of high school conflicts represented more widely in YA fiction.

While the headstrong heroine is not new in culture, iconic female characters from YA books such as Katniss Everdeen or Tris Prior have encouraged a new expectation that women, especially young women, have strength, skill, and stamina enough to save the world. Celaena's drive to be exceptional is not limited to exceptionalism among women; she also desires to be seen as different and better than the men. One of the conditions of her residence at the glass castle is that she must keep her true identity hidden, so that the other competitors will continue to underestimate her. While on a foot race with them, she tells herself, 'She had to stay in the middle. Stay in the middle' (90). This denial of her agency and recognition of her exceptional status leads her to continual frustration: 'I hate you telling me to hold back when … I'm just there, boring and unnoticed in the middle,' she says to Chaol (136). Celaena knows she is better than everyone else, and she is frustrated that this knowledge is not shared more widely.

Another unacknowledged exceptional woman in the text is the dead elven queen, Elena, whose ghost Celaena encounters while exploring one of the castle's secret passageways. The lore of Erilea has remembered Elena, but for the wrong reasons: 'There are many things history has forgotten about me,' she tells Celaena. 'I fought on the battlefields during the demon wars against Erawan – at [elven king] Gavin's side. That's how we fell in love. But your legends portray me as a damsel who waited in a tower with a magic necklace that would help the heroic prince' (398). Elena's words here are a lesson to Celaena in how easily female exceptionalism may be forgotten in a strongly patriarchal, oppressive context such as the pre-modern period, which views men as agential heroes and women as passive damsels. The common medievalist fantasy trope of the exceptional woman allows conflict to arise out of women's resistance to male power.

The Chosen One

The exceptional female hero may also map onto the common fantasy trope of the Chosen One. This trope sees 'heroic destiny' bestowed on a character after that character has been identified by 'a mark, prophecy, auspicious birth, or wise soothsayer' (Chowdhury, 2006: 107). Famous examples from fantasy fiction include Harry Potter, identified by his lightning-bolt scar, or Frodo Baggins, recruited by Gandalf to carry the One Ring. Similarly, while *Throne of Glass* appears at first to be about Celaena's desire to win the competition for her own ends, part way through it is revealed that much more is at stake for the land of Erilea. Elena exhorts her, 'You *must* win this competition . . . Erilea *needs* you' (Maas, 2012: 186). The choice of imperative language such as 'must' and 'needs' (emphasised with italics) firmly underscores the significant stakes involved in Celaena's actions. That significance is tied up in a destiny beyond Celaena's knowledge:

> You must listen to what I tell you. Nothing is a coincidence. Everything has a purpose. You were meant to come to this castle, just as you were meant to be an assassin, to learn the skills necessary for survival . . . You were led here tonight . . . Someone wants you to learn; someone wants you to see. (186–7)

In this prewritten script of her life, Celaena is chosen by 'someone' to fulfil a role in the greater lore of the story because of her exceptional potential. Her other activities until now – for example, her life as an assassin – are all reframed in this moment as belonging to a higher purpose. Her suitability for this higher purpose is embodied in her exceptionalism: 'You could be different . . . You could be great. Greater than me – than any of us' (399). The Chosen One is not only special and different, but also occupies an elevated position, high and powerful enough to 'rattle the stars' (399).

This chosen-for-greatness fantasy narrative has an intensified function when coupled with YA. Michael Levy and Farah Mendlesohn suggest that YA texts are 'intended, in part, to support young people in the belief that their lives *really are important*' (2016: 209), a point that may seem dismissive, but that is worth nuancing and discussing. Adolescence is generally recognised as a period of identity formation, self-fashioning, and self-reflection, which adults may well interpret as self-obsession. In YA fiction, however, these aspects of learning who one is are tied to very high dramatic stakes: they become matters of life or death. In Cassandra Clare's *City of Bones*,

Magnus Bane links adolescent self-obsession directly to Chosen One lore: 'Every teenager in the world feels like that, feels broken or out of place, different somehow, royalty mistakenly born into a family of peasants', underscoring the idea that a period of uncertain identity is directly linked to imaginings of important identity. The lovely irony is that Magnus also tells Clary, 'The difference in your case is that it's true' (2007: 178). While this may seem almost risible – reminding us of the Douglas Adams quotation: 'It's one thing to think that you're the centre of the universe; it's another thing entirely to have this confirmed by an ancient prophecy' (tvtropes 'Chosen') – the genre demands this kind of correspondence between YA identity angst and fantasy's destined-for-greatness inclinations. Young protagonists are often the saviours of fantasy societies precisely because they are young and bring new energy or ideas to the resistance. Magnus's reference to royalty and peasants alerts us, however, to a potentially less positive facet of Chosen One lore: the fact that it is often linked to class and individualism, rather than the kind of equity and collectivism YAF often celebrates in resistance and revolutions; see for example Farah Mendlesohn's 2001 essay on heredity and authority in the *Harry Potter* series. This incongruity alerts us to the ways in which X-meets-Y partnerings of tropes are not always frictionless, and potentially signals a fault line where genre might change over time.

A further specific YA inflection of the fantasy Chosen One trope manifests in the ubiquitous teenage love triangle. The three series under study in this Element all describe such love triangles: Mare in *Red Queen* captures the romantic interest of the two princes, Maven and Cal; Clary in *City of Bones* is beloved by her old friend Simon and the Shadowhunter Jace; and Celaena in *Throne of Glass* attracts both Chaol and Dorian (in subsequent books, Celaena also becomes beloved of fae Prince Rowan). Perhaps the most famous example in YAF is *Twilight*'s Bella Swan, who, despite her self-confessed awkwardness and clumsiness, is pursued by both sparkling, gorgeous vampire Edward and sexy, capable werewolf Jacob. On the surface, these relationships seem to reinforce the Chosen One trope by imagining the female character as being so exceptional that multiple male characters lose their hearts to her. Her confusion and deliberations over these potential relationships are sometimes seen as undermining the gravity of other aspects of the plot: consider Levy and Mendlesohn's observation that YA texts are occupied with the 'belief that one's intimate relationships are essentially more important than the great quests or battles that are taking place out in the world' (2016: 197). However, in many ways, a love triangle presents dualities in the female character's nature, allowing her more complexity and resisting the reduction of ideas to binaries (W. E. Jones, 2014: 64). The female character's appeal to contrasting male suitors may, in fact, show how widely her influence might extend, for example, across mortal and supernatural worlds (Clary in *City of Bones*), warring factions (Bella in *Twilight*), or, in Celaena's case, across race (human Prince Dorian or fae Rowan). A Chosen One has obligations not just to herself and the private world of her heart. The very fact of being chosen implies a far-ranging, public life. That these female characters are 'chosen' by multiple male suitors reinforces, rather than takes away from, their importance to the epic narrative stakes. Consequently, Celaena's (and *Red Queen*'s Mare's and *City of Bones*' Clary's) romantic entanglements, while they contribute to the main narrative of the story, are largely subplots. That is, Celaena and Mare and Clary manage both intimate relationships *and* great quests and battles; *particularly* great quests and battles. Young adult fantasy's exceptional females fulfil at every level the expectations of their Chosen One status. We know this, because they compete and win within and against oppressive institutions.

Tests and Institutions

Fantasy fiction has been repeatedly identified with Joseph Campbell's monomyth, or 'hero's journey', which features a set pattern of narrative events (for example, the 'call to adventure', 'meeting the mentor', and so on). Reading a fantasy story against Campbell's monomyth – where it may be the same and where it may differ – presents us with a similar critical cul-de-sac as taxonomy; indeed, the hero's journey is a form of narrative taxonomy (see for example Palumbo (2005) and Cronn-Mills and Samens (2010)). Such a narrative pattern's repeated appearance in fantasy, especially the epic fantasy subgenre, may be in part related to the genre's taste in pre-modern source material: it is from many pre-modern literary sources, such as the medieval epic *Sir Gawain and the Green Knight*, that Campbell drew his ideas, as did the influential J. R. R. Tolkien. That is, while we cannot say whether or not writers have deliberately applied the monomyth, we can say they acquire a genre competence through reading that may mean the monomyth has correspondent features with their texts. So while I gesture towards Campbell here, I do so with caution, always aware that genre is not a slavish following of rules, but a constant negotiation between those invested in the genre, whether they be writers, readers, or publishers.

Of special interest for contemporary fantasy fiction is the stage of the journey that Campbell called 'a succession of trials. This is a favourite phase of the myth-adventure. It has produced a world literature of miraculous tests and ordeals ... Dragons have now to be slain and surprising barriers passed – again, again, and again' (1949: 81). The language of 'trials' and 'tests' is associated here with repeated pleasure ('favourite', 'again'). The genre's interest in a succession of trials lends fantasy novels their distinctive narrative shape: the doorstop text with an extended middle made up of small servings of dramatic interest (defeating escalating supernatural and/or violent threats), often on the way to facing a larger, defining supernatural and/or violent threat. In many cases, this proliferation of trials carries over into subsequent books, lending the genre to seriality (see Section 3). Young adult fantasy is particularly apposite for representing such trials for a number of reasons.

First, trials are linked to the adolescent 'rite of passage'; that is, the tests exist in 'an intertextual field of inference' that adds layers of significance to the hero's actions. Ultimately, passing the trials is part of the overarching narrative of 'restoring or redefining the world' (Driscoll and Heatwole, 2017: 271). Second, tests and trials are part of a contemporary frame of reference for adolescents. As Alexander and Black argue, '[w]ith standardised testing occupying such a prominent place in contemporary educational contexts it is not surprising that various manifestations of high stakes testing have made their way into popular fiction for young adults' (2015: 208). The image of 'high stakes testing' is everywhere in YAF, even if the stakes do not appear, at first, to be high. The Hogwarts Sorting Hat may seem a relatively benign form of testing, but it does play a role in the inter-house rivalry that drives a great deal of the drama of the *Harry Potter* series. In adolescents' real lives, high-stakes testing often implies competition, and

YAF books 'emphasise the ubiquity of competition, offering us worlds in which young people must learn to fight, often one another, in order to survive' (Alexander and Black, 2015: 213). Third, the physically demanding and often violent nature of the tests may stand in figuratively for the 'sometimes wrenching physical, emotional and intellectual changes' of adolescence (Levy and Mendlesohn, 2016: 204). For many of these fantasy tests and trials, young characters must physically transform: Celaena, for example, trains so hard that her 'body screams' and she sometimes throws up afterwards (Maas, 2012: 94, 104). She refers to herself as 'out of shape' in the early training for the Tests, but over time gets stronger and faster, showing the way 'female, heroic bodies' may represent transformation through 'instability, change and, even injury' (Phillips, 2015: 44). The physically transformative power of partaking in a succession of trials links metaphorically to the physical transformations of young adulthood.

The various stages in the competition that governs the action in *Throne of Glass* are explicitly called 'Tests' (Maas, 2012: 88), a word used in every secondary school environment. Moreover, the adolescent inflection of the competition is underscored by some of the adjacent adolescent concerns that Celaena expresses, for instance, when period pain interferes with her training ('Celaena groaned. How was she going to train like this?' (254)), or when Prince Dorian arrives at her chamber with romantic intentions and she rebuffs him with 'What are you doing here? It's almost midnight and I've got a Test tomorrow' (227), or when she counts down with dread to the competition deadline: 'There were only nine weeks left until the final duel, and some of the others ... were doing well enough that those four spots were starting to seem rather precious' (159). Each competitor has a trainer (Celaena's is Chaol), and training takes place under the seasoned warrior Theodus Brullo: 'I've been Weapons Master here for thirty years ... I've trained many a lord and knight – and many a would-be Champion of Adarlan. It will be *very* hard to impress me' (85). His age and his experience, as well as his ability to shape the destinies of the competitors (deciding the difference between would-be Champions and real Champions), mean that he functions very much like a senior authority figure at a school, with the power and knowledge to force obedience. Celaena has had an even more demanding educational experience before, though, with Arobynn, who 'trained me himself, and then brought in tutors from all over Erilea', and would have 'flogged her' for not achieving highly (157). Celaena's power and agency as an assassin are shown to have been the product, at every step, of a demanding and punitive educational system. This educational system has been either directly oppressive, or is linked to larger oppressive social structures.

Alexander and Black show that representation of high-stakes testing in YAF is always linked to social control: 'The types of people, forms of learning, and skills and strategies being cultivated are clear indicators of the cultural values of the governments represented in these novels' (2015: 212). In *Throne of Glass*, the King's Assassin role is linked to maintaining the king's power in Erilea, as Dorian puts it: 'His *Champion* would keep his opponents quiet' (Maas, 2012: 15). The king's regime, however, is brutal and oppressive: indeed, it was under this system that Celaena entered the salt mines in the first place. The deal she has made, that she can only be free if she serves the king, proves that she is not free at all. She must either be oppressed or oppressor – 'a fang in the mouth of the beast' (16) – against her own moral judgement. Again, while the oppressive regime is not a trope unique to young adult expressions of fantasy, there is nonetheless a privileged relationship between adolescents and resistance to authority that gives the trope extra salience. Alexander and Black 'read such regimes psychoanalytically as stand-ins for "parental figures"' (2015: 227–8), while Alkestrand suggests that the fantastic mode 'permit[s] the books to criticise the power that adults have over adolescents, both as individuals and institutions' (2014: 110).

Resistance to institutions on an epic scale – nations or worlds – is a mainstay of fantasy fiction that sees full expression in YAF. Celaena may end the first volume in the *Throne of Glass* series with the idea that, after her term as King's Assassin, she will 'begin again – far away from Adarlan. She could go away and forget this awful kingdom' (Maas, 2012: 402). But as early as chapter two of the second book, *Crown of Midnight*, she is hiding the truth about who she has assassinated, and playing a '*very* lethal game' by deepening ties with the rebels (Maas, 2013: 6, 16). Ultimately, as the series progresses, she becomes a leader and war hero of immense magical and physical power. The shift from concerns about self to concerns about the safety of whole nations is common in YAF series (see also *Red Queen*), raising the stakes from one book to the next. The first in a series often represents a heroine who is exceptional at what Tolmie would call 'excelling within the system': Celaena absolutely fulfils this definition; resisting the physical and legal oppression of men is her 'female agenda' in *Throne of Glass* (2006: 155). But YAF is nearly always published in series. In the ten or so years since Tolmie wrote her influential essay, YAF has reset the horizons for fantasy heroines and, indeed, for the gender of oppressors: from *Heir of Fire*, Queen Maeve becomes Celaena/Aelin's chief persecutor. Female heroes in YAF are 'empowered beyond what a normal teenager could hope for' (Alkestrand, 2014: 115). In most cases, they bring that power to positions of morally just leadership against oppression and injustice, opening up the pre-modern oppressive setting, to prove the worthiness of the chosen hero.

Conclusion

Fantasy's genre tropes are well known and, we may assume from the fact that they still attract a large audience, well loved. The young adult inflection of these tropes adds new resonance and new appeal for a changing audience in a new century. The pre-modern setting finds new energy when giving young female characters a chance to demonstrate their agency against oppressive and dangerous social structures. The Chosen One convention seems a particularly useful prism to view adolescent characters discovering their identities and their purpose. Magical trials are a way of dramatising the high-stakes testing that concerns adolescent audiences. A study of the textual aspects of YAF, especially the enduring conventions of high fantasy, suggests the way that genres can change over time under the shaping pressure of audiences and the industry that seeks to attract those audiences.

2 Originality and the Social

Both Series feature mortal or normal objects (referred to as 'instruments' by the DEFENDANT), including without limitation a cup, a sword, and a mirror, each imbued with magical properties to help battle evil and protect mankind. The character's powers are heightened or restrained by the use of supernatural markings. Both Dark-Hunters and Shadowhunters have enchanted swords that are divinely forged, imbued with other-worldly spirits, have unique names, and glow like heavenly fire. (*Kenyon* v. *Clare*, Case 3:16-cv-00191, 2016)

This excerpt from the copyright infringement complaint brought by Sherrilyn Kenyon against Cassandra Clare provides us the incongruity of seeing genre conventions – magical objects and supernatural battles – in legal documents, rather than their usual reading and entertainment environment. Such incongruity suggests that genre conventions do not operate solely textually: they shape and are shaped by discussion, debate, and disagreement; they can even be entered into evidence in a court of law. That is, genres have a social dimension.

This section takes as its central focus the *social* aspects of YAF, investigating not only the way that genres form and set expectations of social groupings, especially fandoms, but also the way that those social groupings then set expectations and police genres. The theme of this section is originality, and so it asks questions about how far genre tropes can be reproduced before they exhaust an audience's patience with the same thing, and what some of the indicators of that exhaustion might look like. It also shows that audiences are not all of one mind on this mix of what is replayed in genre and what is left in play – far from it – and how these disagreements are productive in themselves of the discourses that shape genres.

City of Bones, the first in Cassandra Clare's ongoing *The Mortal Instruments* series (sometimes called, more controversially, the *Shadowhunters* series: see later in this Element), follows the initiation of unconventional New York teenager Clary Fray into an underground supernatural group who hunt and kill demons. When Clary's mother goes missing, Clary confronts a world of monsters that exists alongside the ordinary world, and learns that she is no ordinary teenager and her parentage is, too, extraordinary. She struggles with conflicting feelings about her long-time friend Simon and the brooding Shadowhunter Jace, and uses her courage and intellect to unlock long-buried memories and to solve the mystery of her mother's disappearance. Similar YAF texts include Maggie Stiefvater's *The Raven Boys* and Laini

Taylor's *Daughter of Smoke and Bone*, both of which also feature real-world settings and unconventional young protagonists with special abilities, and borrow from European mythology. Both have also been optioned for film and television adaptations. Clare's text is particularly suitable for a discussion about the social dimensions of YAF, as Clare performed her writing apprenticeship in fan communities, and has subsequently been a lightning rod for controversy in fandom.

Sometime between the first edition of *City of Bones* and the 2015 edition that I own, Clare added a foreword about her sources, both popular and classical, to frame her use of mythological ideas and beings. Whether this addition was an artistic decision for a new edition or a response to the insistent allegations of lack of originality on Clare's part cannot be known. What the change alerts us to, though, is that the author hopes to shape our reading experience and to lead us into a particular frame for understanding her use of YAF genre elements. However, many readers have pushed back against Clare, and fannish audiences have created their own frame for this understanding, to the point where fans' impulse to police the genre they love has informed legal action against Clare for copyright infringement. This section considers the way Clare, who rose from fandom herself, sets out a vision of passionate reading and writing. It also considers the way that fandom has responded with defences of Clare and with discontent, and the interactions between genre and law.

Passionate Reading and Writing

Reading in *City of Bones*, according to Clary's mother, is a 'sacred pastime' (Clare, 2007: 34), a phrase that alerts us to the specific and elevated investments in books and bookishness that are evident in the text. Collections of books gather in important places: Clary's beloved stepfather, Luke, owns a bookstore, her (sometimes) helpful psychic neighbour, Madame Dorothea, has an apartment full of magic books (111), and the description of Clary's first visit to the Institute's library is long and rapturous:

> The walls were lined with books, the shelves so high that tall
> ladders set on casters were placed along them at intervals.
> These were no ordinary books either – these were books

> bound in leather and velvet, clasped with sturdy-looking
> locks and hinges made of brass and silver. (77)

The language of height and size are used here to give a sense of sublime scale, while the tactile descriptions (leather, velvet, sturdy, brass, silver) bring the protagonist into close, embodied proximity. Clary's positive response to the sight of the library is noted by Hodge, who cites "'[t]he look on your face when you walked in'" as a visible and personal indicator that she is a 'book lover' (78). The books themselves, in Clary's opinion, 'had been loved', a fact that seems directly related to their status as 'no ordinary books' (77). These books are special, and the ability to recognise and appreciate that specialness indicates a potential specialness in the lover. After all, Madame Dorothea's library of magical books, according to Jace, is not special enough. "'There's not one serious text here,'" he says contemptuously. Rather the shelves are full of the "'trash she keeps ... to impress credible mundanes'" (113). Implied here is the idea that books can function as a way to sort people socially into knowledgeable in-groups and ignorant out-groups: those who understand what a valuable, important, even magical book really is, and those who are too readily impressed by fakery.

The act of writing in *City of Bones* is also used to identify in- and out-groups. Clary's old school friend Simon is in a social group with an aspiring poet named Eric, whose writing is considered unintentionally comical by the characters and is presented as humour to the readers: "'*Come, my faux juggernaut, my nefarious loins! Slather every protuberance with arid zeal!*'" (50). By contrast, Jace and the other Shadowhunters use a magical runic language derived from angels: in another book of magic, a grimoire, "'is copied every rune the Angel Raziel wrote in the original Book of the Covenant ... Some of the runes are so powerful they'd burn through regular pages'" (248). The Shadowhunters use magical writing instruments called steles to draw the 'matrix of swirling lines' on their skin (20), powerfully and agentially: 'iratze' is for healing (106), 'voyance' is for seeing (54), and so on. But for Clare, the power of writing goes beyond a direct correspondence with runic letters and magical acts. In her foreword, Clare states that her protagonist is 'an artist and a shaper of runes' who uses 'that language' to shape 'her own story and her own destiny' (2015: iii).

Powerful claims are made in the text and in the foreword for the deliberate and formidable potential of writing in the hands of the special people such as artists and Shadowhunters, while elsewhere, other characters, like Eric, are only capable of '"vomiting up words at random"' (Clare, 2007: 53).

The characters' investments in reading and writing are in some ways a reflection of Clare's own investment, as expressed in the foreword. 'When I set out to write *City of Bones*, I was in love with stories about vampires and faeries and warlocks, but I was also in love with the mythological tales of angels and demons.' Clare writes here of love of particular ideas, the conjunction 'but' suggesting two varieties of them. The first is a love of 'stories': as vampires, faeries, and warlocks are conventions of contemporary urban fantasy, she refers here to popular fiction like her own. The second is a love of 'mythological tales' among which she includes highbrow texts such as Milton's *Paradise Lost* and Dante's *Inferno* (Clare, 2015: i). In this short declaration of her passionate investments, Clare explicitly links supernatural stories from both popular and classical sources. It is the conventions that engender her 'love' no matter which point on the spectrum of artistic value she draws from. She also shows that these supernatural creatures of popular culture have a literary heritage, that in some ways they are linked to the special books and writing that are at the heart of the extraordinary nature of the Shadowhunters, and provides her readers with a glimpse, perhaps even an invitation, into the world of 'mythological tales' that the bestselling fiction they read is based on.

Clare is very aware of her reading community, or her 'fandom', and social relationships in the text share a similar logic of community, mediated through the understanding of literature (as we have seen) but also popular media. Fannish acts are interwoven with the action from the very first scene, where a teenage boy enters the nightclub Pandemonium in cosplay, dressed as a 'vampire hunter' and armed with a 'fake' foam-rubber stake (Clare, 2007: 14). This character is actually a vampire, playing a human, playing a vampire hunter. His arrival functions as the inciting incident for Clary's initiation into the world of the Shadowhunters, so it is not a trivial plot point. A cosplaying vampire hunter mediates Clary's introduction into the storyworld, just as fannish knowledge about cosplay and vampire hunters mediates the readers'.

Investments in fandom also provide characters with reference points about how to make sense of the circumstances they find themselves in. Simon warns Clary that he has learned from playing *Dungeons and Dragons* that it is "'usually better not to mess with powerful objects'" (Clare, 2007: 352); Clary makes the decision to stand back to back in a combat scene because "'[i]n movies that's what they do in this kind of ... situation'" (297), and Simon judges masculine behaviour by comparing what he sees to the comic book superhero interactions of Wolverine and Magneto (360).

This fannish knowledge, however, is surpassed by the actual supernatural knowledge of the Shadowhunters. When 'mundie' Simon mentions *Dungeons and Dragons* to Shadowhunter Jace, Clary is 'vaguely embarrassed' to explain that it is a game where "'[p]eople pretend to be wizards and elves and they kill monsters and stuff'" (Clare, 2007: 129). Simon's misunderstandings about supernatural creatures are contrasted with Jace's first-hand knowledge: "'dragons [are] mostly extinct ... Real elves are about eight inches tall'" (130). As Clary's power grows, so does her experiential knowledge, to the point where Simon's fannish metaphors begin to annoy her: "'It's not a funny game where the worst thing that happens is you get a bad dice roll'" (353). A clear line is drawn between enthusiasts who 'pretend' and those who experience the reality. In one sense, it is a trick of Clare's craft, to make her world seem more real by disavowing the generic fan tropes that precede it (while also using them). But it also starts the work of separating characters into those on the inside with knowledge, and those on the outside with only their enthusiasm. Clare links this distinction between insiders and outsiders with perspective, especially perspectives related to artistic expression.

Early in the text, we see Clary drawing a picture of a 'dark prince ... astride his black steed, his sable cape flowing behind him. A golden circlet bound his blond locks, his handsome face was cold with the rage of battle' (Clare, 2007: 30). The generic nature of this drawing is apparent: she is drawing a stock fantasy character, the kind of subject matter often seen in fan art. Clary is frustrated with her limitations as an artist and perhaps with the limitations of stock fantasy characters: 'The drawing just wasn't working. With a sigh, she tore yet another sheet from her sketchpad ... Already the floor was littered with discarded balls of paper' (30). This well-used trope of the artist balling up failed drawing after failed drawing indicates the amount of time and effort she invests in the practice. Yet it is only after her many encounters with actual fantasy characters that her skills in drawing lead to more than just 'good picture[s]', but *magical* pictures: 'She'd caught the hard line of [Jace's] mouth, the incongruously vulnerable eyes. The wings looked so real . . . Her fingers had touched not dry paper but the soft down of feathers' (341). With Clary's new and powerful control of her art comes the solution to the riddle of the missing Mortal Cup: Clary's mother had painted it into a tarot card (369). Outside of the Shadowhunters' world is Simon's fannish misunderstandings and Clary's failed drawings of fantasy warriors. Inside is real supernatural characters and art that can transcend two-dimensional representation and become real.

Luke prefigures Clary's connection between art and a special perspective early in the text, when he tells her that she is '"an artist like your mother. That means you see the world in ways that other people don't"' (Clare, 2007: 35). Already, early in the book, Clary ('you') is being separated out from the rank and file of 'other people' through her ability to see differently. Her unique perspective is one of the ways the Shadowhunters eventually recognise that Clary is not a '"stupid little mundie"' as the imperious Isabelle calls her at first meeting (26). The word is short for 'mundane', and describes '"Someone of the human world"' or a non-magical person (53). But as Jace notes, '"You seem to be a mundane like any other mundane, yet you can see me. It's a conundrum"' (53) – a conundrum that leads him to quiz her on her knowledge of the supernatural world: '"Have you had dealings with demons, little girl? Walked with warlocks, talked with the Night Children?"' (27). The alliteration and capitalisation make his words seem almost like a nursery rhyme, and his use of the term 'little girl' is intended to diminish her and her experiences, even though they are the same age. With his language, he shows that he speaks from a position of mature knowledge, of things she cannot possibly know.

But Clary can see what 'Mundies' cannot, opening up the division between her old friendship with Simon and her new relationships with the Shadowhunters. The first time she takes Simon to the Institute, he says, '"this place is a dump,"' but Clary can see through the 'glamour' or magic spell of perspective to what is really underneath: 'the true vision glowing through the false one like light through dark glass . . . The soaring spires of the cathedral, the dull gleam of the leaded windows . . . ' (Clare, 2007: 146). Similarly, when a black car comes to fetch her, she can 'pierce the veil of the glamour' and see something else entirely:

> Now the car looked like Cinderella's carriage, except instead of being pink and gold and blue like an Easter egg, it was black as velvet, its windows darkly tinted. The wheels were black, the leather trimmings all black. On the black metal driver's bench sat Brother Jeremiah, holding a set of reins in parchment-coloured robes. On the other end of the reins were two horses, black as smoke, snarling and pawing at the sky. (185)

Clare moves here from the innocence of fairy tales and childhood treats to dark, tactile descriptions: the word 'black' is used five times, and velvet, leather, metal, parchment, and smoke as a group of materials invoke (and potentially knit together) both the traditional gothic genre (velvet, parchment, smoke) and contemporary expressions of the gothic across media (leather, metal, and, yes, velvet, which it should be noted is not necessarily black, as Clare claims, except in this genre), including urban fantasy. The wildness of the barely tamed animals, whose energy will be used to drive the carriage, literalises the car's 'horsepower'. Mundies see a black car; those with special perspective see a tableau of strangely beautiful darkness and movement. That this tableau is thoroughly generic is meaningful here: one of the complaints about the value of genre fiction is that, from an outside perspective, it all looks very ordinary in its sameness. One of the defences from the inside perspective is that there is beauty and power in the infinite nuanced variations of expressing the familiar.

This ability to see what others cannot is linked to power, especially the power of surveillance. When Jace draws a viewing portal in a screen he and Clary are hiding behind, he mouths to her '*They can't see us through it, but we can see them*' (Clare, 2007: 136). The line between 'us' and 'them' is drawn, and it is a line of knowledge but also judgement: Clary immediately equates the portal with the 'one-way' glass in interrogation rooms. 'We' can see and judge while remaining unseen and unjudged: a logic that maps easily onto the earlier scene of Clary spotting two girls on the train with 'pink jelly mules and fake tans', the 'sort of girls Clary had never liked'. She fears at first they are laughing at her, but then realises they are not looking at her at all (97–8). These girls are the 'them,' on the outside of perspective, being watched without being aware they are being watched, and being silently judged with it.

The reason I have spent so long establishing that the text is concerned with the social affinities of in-groups and out-groups, and that the divisions between them are drawn by perspective and knowledge of special texts and art, is that in many ways, *City of Bones* prefigures the logic of the fandom that has gathered around it. The sniping about Mundies and freaks mimics fandom's 'wank', as fandom's dramas and disagreements are collectively known. Jace's series of challenging questions to Clary and his dismissive 'little girl' echo the debates about 'fake geek girls' in certain fandoms, especially in highly gendered video game and comic book fandoms. The text represents a version of the fannish readers and their world, intensifying and tightening identification between characters and audience. Of course, not every reader of *The Mortal Instruments* is a fan – there is always the potential for a neutral reading or even a 'hate reading' of Clare's work – but Clare's authorial identity inarguably has become inseparable from the idea of YAF fandoms. As fellow YAF author Maggie Stiefvater points out, 'Cassie has a fandom, and I still mostly have readers. She is generally seen as a creator, and I am seen as an author' (in Bell, 2015: np). Clare's large and passionate fandom could be related to the televisual adaptations of her work, to the franchise-like nature of her books about Shadowhunters, or to her own personal history as passionate fan herself, which gives her an insider's view on how to position herself and her authorial persona for fandom. Clare's reputation as a fan is largely based on the 3,000-page fan fiction *The Draco Trilogy*, written under the name Cassandra Claire (with an i), which cultivated a very large readership inside Harry Potter fandom many years before her publication via a more traditional route as Cassandra Clare (Jamison, 2013: 233). This history places the acquisition of genre competence and the development of her writing craft squarely within fandom.

Young Adult Fantasy Fandom and Its Discontents

Fandoms exist for many different pursuits; for example, football fandoms are some of the largest and most passionate collections of fans imaginable. However, fandom is generally understood to mean fans of genre books, movies, games, comics, and so on. Young adult fantasy fandoms are particularly engaged forms of fandom, and reveal the social life of books that sales data can never capture: YAF fandoms prove unequivocally that people do more with books than simply buy them and read them. 'Contemporary book cultures', as Steiner calls the range of engaged book-based activities, have turned readers 'into prosumers' (2015: 23); that is, YAF fandom not only consumes the genre, it also helps to constitute it through discussion, elaboration, and amateur creativity.

Book industry analysts the Codex group affirm that urban fantasy fandoms, Clare's subgenre, display 'loyalty levels' that are 'intensely high compared to just about any other fiction category' (in Green, 2016: np). The fantasy genre has always had a privileged relationship with fandom. Henry Jenkins has traced the origins of fandom back to the 'letter columns of Hugo Gernsback's *Amazing Stories*', a dedicated speculative fiction magazine that commenced publication in the 1920s. In the letters pages, readers were encouraged to discuss and debate the stories. Jenkins holds, then, that speculative fiction, of which fantasy is the most commercially lucrative subset, has historically always 'maintained close ties' between writers and their readers and has always expected 'intelligent user criticism' (2014: 40). 'Fans are fans,' according to Hills, because they engage in '[a]nalysis, interpretation, and speculation, building a community through shared texts and playfully appropriating them for their own ends' (2002: 138). Readers, such as those whom Maggie Stiefvater claims as her audience, simply read, whereas fans, like Clare's audience, 'expand the experience of the text beyond its initial consumption' through 'a social process' of interpretation via discussion (Jenkins, 2014: 39). Fandoms are, in their most essential sense, communities. Fandom is 'the fans' universe' (B. Jones, 2014: 2.3), a group of people joined by their intense 'sense of possessiveness, ownership and textual attachments' (Hills, 2002: 35).

In recent years, the ability to build fan communities has become more and more readily facilitated in digital spaces. Websites and connections proliferate in an online environment (Schwabach, 2009: 420), bearing out Hills's assertion that 'online fandoms cannot merely be viewed as a version of "offline" fandoms' but are rather remediated, with their own specific complexions. For example, to post as a fan online is to speak to a potential large and global audience, many members of which will not be personally known to the poster. The possibilities to share in fannish pleasure are vastly expanded. The online space also offers potential freedom from organised events and official facilitators: fans may post opinions outside moderated forums – for example, their own blogs or social media – and thus resist 'any controlling or synthesising gaze' (Hills, 2002: 137). Online fandoms also know that 'other fans will act as a readership for speculations, observations and commentaries', thus creating and consuming 'a textual construction' of the fandom along with the original text around which fans gather (139), while also mirroring 'the fan's attachment back to him or her, validating the affective experience itself' (143). As David Wright notes, 'the language of liking, disliking and sharing' permeates online environments, while entertainment media, including books, are 'a significant part of how ... digital media technologies are lived with and used' (2015: 145). Connecting via sharing opinions about books online has become ubiquitous; the Internet is a powerful tool for user participation.

The sentiments fans express online are not always of earnest pleasure; fans may also express judgement or negativity. Maggie Stiefvater notes that 'the Internet climate seems to have shifted ... to a place where being enthusiastic and positive is no longer cool,' while Clare blames the speed of social media platforms such as Twitter in encouraging 'snap judgements and witch hunts. Everything happens so fast there's not time to check facts or moderate virulence' (in Bell, 2015: np). Sometimes a YA social media storm arises for noble reasons, such as to protest the way minorities are represented in texts. Advanced reading copies of Keira Drake's *The Continent* attracted social media accusations of racism, which culminated in an online petition for HarperTeen to delay the book's publication until it had undergone 'additional editorial focus on the troubling portrayals within of people of color and native backgrounds'. HarperTeen was put in the position of agreeing to push back the publication date of a book for which it had paid upwards of $250,000, by more than a year, to 'ensure that the themes in [Drake's] book are communicated in the way she planned' (thepetitionsite.com).

Evidence reveals that the audience for YA is more likely to be on the Internet. For example, while *Goodreads* ratings are fairly 'equally distributed' across genres, Verboord shows that YA fiction still receives more reviews than other genres (2011: 453). This more active engagement alerts us to young readers' strongly held investments, which drive them to share their opinions (of the 1.4 million reviews of *City of Bones* on *Goodreads*, nearly half are five stars: unequivocal endorsement). Their active engagement is also likely due to the fact that they are '"native speakers' of the digital language of . . . the Internet' (Prensky, 2001: 1): young adults, having grown up with the interoperability of Web 2.0, 'have adopted the Internet as a way to find information, talk to friends and follow trends' more than any other age demographic (Verboord, 2011: 456). They also produce responses to texts in the form of fan fiction, or fic. Writing of what Michael Saler calls the 'communal elaboration' common to audiences for fantasy fiction (2012: 90), one critic labels fic as 'the first digitally native fiction' (Green, 2016: np). At the date of writing, the top three texts adapted on fanfiction.net, the world's largest fan fiction site, were all YAF: *Harry Potter* (with 802,000 stories), followed by *Twilight* (220,000) and *Percy Jackson and the Olympians* (75,800). Clare's own series, *The Mortal Instruments*, comes in at number seven, with a relatively modest 17,600 fics (i.e., fan fiction responses) written about it. According to Roth and Flegel, 'the tenacious narrative of the singular genius and the passive consumer' is inadequate to the task of describing fandom's creative investments (2013: 204). These fics and other fan creative responses to texts such as fan art are as much a part of the YAF genre as the traditionally published texts themselves. The communities that gather around them are also a sensitive barometer of YAF's investments and discontents.

While fans are oriented towards sharing and reciprocity, which is how they 'create and cement [a fandom's] social structure' (B. Jones, 2014: 2.3), this is not the whole story of fandom. As Hills points out, a fandom is also '*a social hierarchy* where fans share common interests while also competing over fan knowledge, access to the object of fandom, and status' (2002: 20).

Clare's own history as a fan bears out this idea: in Harry Potter fic fandom, she was a big-name fan or BNF – 'the very biggest name of all', according to Jamison (2013: 233) – and thus a possessor of much 'fan social capital' (Hills, 2002: 30). As an author, she now has her own fandom, made up mostly of 'young girls and women' (Clare in Bell, 2015: np). The Codex research bears this out, finding that Clare's 'peak audience is women ages 18 to 24, among whom she's as popular as Gwyneth Paltrow and Cameron Diaz' (in Green, 2016: np). She is often considered part of her own fandom, perhaps because she started as a fan, or perhaps because she is 'really available' to her fans. She says, though, that this 'imbalance of power' between her and her readers 'breeds an awful tension. I have never seen that not happen. I have never seen any author . . . who has been able to prevent it' (in Bell, 2015: np). In some instances, fans turn on the authors whose works they love: 'They talk about how much they love the work, but they hate you personally, sometimes intensely, specifically for being the person who has control over the characters' (in Bell, 2015: np).

Fandoms, then, can respond in different ways to texts, to their creators, and to the discussions around them (Jamison, 2013: 232). Clare acknowledges fans 'are not a monolith – they don't all prioritise the same characters, or want the same things, or even like the same things about a story' (in Bell, 2015: np), flagging that disagreements are invariably about the content and interpretation of texts. Within these discussions, even the author is not immune to criticism. Fans' sense of possessiveness over Clare's characters can lead them to 'turn on her for plot directions they don't approve of', a phenomenon sometimes called 'fantitlement' (Green, 2016: np). Fan disagreements can seem petty and trivial to those outside fandoms, leading Elizabeth Minkel and Laura Miller to agree that the controversy surrounding Clare is reminiscent of the drama of high school (Miller, 2016: np). In sum, unequal access to social capital and different positions in the hierarchy, combined with intense attachments to texts and opinions about texts, with the extra factor of the social inexperience of youth, can mean that fandom is brimming with 'competitive, argumentative, and factional possibilities' (Hills, 2002: xvii). Clare has proven this assertion, attracting some of the most ferocious 'wank' among fan communities, around fic, originality, and plagiarism: all things that relate back to genre.

It is difficult to find online an account of the Clare controversy, popularly referred to as 'Cassiegate', where a subjective voice does not potentially skew interpretation. The most famous and longest account, by a blogger named Avocado, is now only available via The WayBack Machine, an Internet archiving site. Avocado admits in their first paragraph, 'As you read, you may say, "Your grudge is showing"' (2006: np). Indeed, objectivity is difficult to find in any account, but Anne Jamison's work on fic covers the major points relatively neutrally (2013: 232–9). Clare, writing under the pen-name Cassandra Claire, became famous in Harry Potter fandom for her trilogy of fic about Draco Malfoy. As well as repurposing J. K. Rowling's characters (as fic does), Claire sprinkled the stories with multiple popular culture references: for example, jokes and lines from cult TV shows *Buffy the Vampire Slayer* and *Babylon 5*. These she acknowledged in an author note at the start of her fics with a nudge-wink, almost a game to see if readers could spot them: a classic act of fannish social affinity testing, echoed in Jace's challenging interrogation of Clary's knowledge of the supernatural world cited earlier. But unacknowledged sections of an out-of-print fantasy text by Pamela Dean were also written into *The Draco Trilogy*. Claire was accused of plagiarism and, despite her enormous following on fanfiction.net, her work was taken down and she was banned. Clare (the published author) has explained that she may have written down the lines because she liked them then later forgot they were not hers: a reasonable enough explanation for somebody who reads and writes as much as Clare does. Wank ensued and two camps formed very quickly: those who did not like Claire (the fic writer) found many other reasons to insist she was a plagiarist; those who did like Claire excused her and wanted her stories to return. Others took to forums to say that Claire was now cyberbullying them, playing the angry respondent who could not 'moderate' her 'virulence', to use her own words cited earlier in this Element. Clare denies these accusations and has since become an outspoken critic of cyberbullying (2012). Clare, now associated with plagiarism, has since faced accusations that her *The Mortal Instruments* series is actually Harry Potter fic 'with the serial numbers filed off', a common expression among fic forums.

Accusations of unoriginality are paradoxical: as Schwabach tells us, fic is 'necessarily derivative; it cannot function otherwise' (2009: 398). However, the concept of unoriginality is central to this controversy. Note that *City of Bones* and the series it belongs to could not in any way be seen as a version of *The Draco Trilogy*, unlike E. L. James's megaselling *Fifty Shades of Grey*, which started as a *Twilight* fic called *Masters of the Universe*. While it has been speculated that the characters of Jace and Clary draw heavily from Clare's fic representations of Draco Malfoy and Ginny Weasley, the only direct transposition of text is one small scene in *City of Bones* where Jace recounts his father killing his beloved falcon (Clare, 2007: 220–2), which is a story Draco tells in the fic (and which has no antecedent at all in the *Harry Potter* series). However, Clare's detractors repeatedly cite her copying of *Harry Potter* as a reason to condemn her and her work. The following comments are all taken from the same *Goodreads* discussion page. Keshena writes: 'Any similarities between MI and HP are not coincidental at all! Cassandra Clare is a huge Potterphile,' while Gabby agrees: 'Cassandra Clare origionally [*sic*] wrote this as a fanfiction of Harry Potter.' Mimi points to Clare's known history as an alleged plagiarist as evidence that *The Mortal Instruments* cannot be entirely original: 'If Clare had never written Harry Potter fan fiction and had never plagiarised, then no one would be accusing her of a crime, but because she did those two things, it kind of opens up the real light of her "inspiration"' (Various, 2012: np). Mimi assumes that Clare's 'inspiration' is Harry Potter, rather than the more likely scenario that Clare and J. K. Rowling draw similar inspiration in a shared reading history of other fantasy texts and mythological tales. It appears that Clare has breached a social code in fandom, and the attendant anxiety about her switch from fic writer to fiction writer continues to frame the response of various social groups whose fandom knowledge is high.

Genre and the Law

Stepping out of the role of fan and into the role of bestselling author provokes fan backlash for a number of reasons, and fic is a good barometer of these reasons. In the *Twilight* fandom debates that followed the publication and extraordinary success of E. L. James's *Fifty Shades* series, many of these reasons became apparent, and they relate to the way that social cohesion is maintained in fandoms. The reputation of fandom and fic writers in the wider community is at stake. Jones cites fans complaining that 'pulling to publish', or converting fic into commercial published outcomes, 'makes every last one of us look bad' because it confirms a stereotype of fic writers 'leaching off the real creativity of others' (2014:1.4). Also important is the preservation of a 'gift economy' in fandom, where fan production happens within a supportive environment, including 'the freely given input' of readers who help fic writers to 'refine works'. When those works are used to 'get a step up' into the market and the fan gift economy is left behind, trust is betrayed (3.4). On top of this, fan hierarchies are disrupted or the discontents over them sharpened. On a *Goodreads* thread about Clare's alleged questionable originality, one participant, Mist Cassidy, defends Clare by suggesting that her transition from fan to bestselling author was at the root of the wank: 'people that claimed she was a copycat, were all haters who were jealous that Cassandra was living her dream and they weren't' (Various, 2012: np). Clare herself acknowledges that the transition made her seem 'uppity' to some in fandom (in Green, 2016: np).

As well as these compelling social reasons to condemn 'pulling to publish', there are imagined legal reasons for fandom to police this practice. Fans are concerned that fic writers who pivot to high-profile publishing careers may arouse suspicion that fic is profiting from copyright infringement. The fear is that writers of original works will prohibit fic, and so fans police copyright and originality with a lay understanding of copyright law. They prosecute this socially formed or 'folk' notion of copyright law 'based on the *fan community's* interpretation and understanding of their legal rights' (Roth and Flegel, 2013: 209). These folk notions may include practices such as disclaimers in forewords, and maintaining (and policing) not-for-profit ambitions for fan works, a key factor they believe engenders the 'toleration by rightsholders' of fic (Jamison, 2013: 234). Within this folk understanding of copyright, it is easy to see how the fic-related plagiarism accusations against Clare represent a potentially 'catastrophically reckless sin against the entire community' (Miller, 2016: np). While copyright infringement and plagiarism are two very different things – copyright infringement is a failure to secure permission to use somebody else's work; plagiarism is passing off someone else's work as your own without attribution – the two are often conflated in fandom's socially determined legal understanding. Author John Scalzi has been scathing in his linking of fic to plagiarism: 'really, if you're *already* wantonly violating copyright, what's a little *plagiarism* to go along with it? Honestly. In for a penny, in for a pound' (2006). It is against these stereotypes that YAF fic writers need to defend themselves. 'Pulling to publish' threatens a community that believes it is legally safe to continue enjoying fan elaboration of their favourite works, and so the behaviour is policed in the best way fandom knows: through a 'pile-on' of fan discontent and wank, demonstrating fans' 'desire to maintain their rules within their community' (Roth and Flegel, 2013: 211–12). The originality or otherwise of Clare's work, then, is policed by fandom as though it is of very high significance.

In an instance of this community policing in the same *Goodreads* thread cited earlier in this Element, a poster named Mimi lists the 'coincidences' between Rowling's and Clare's series:

> Mundies: Muggles
> Valentine and Voldemort have nearly the same goal
> Everyone thought Valentine/Voldemort was dead at the
>   beginning
> Shadowhunters and wizards are WAY to[o] alike
> The Clave is a cheap knock off of the Ministry of Magic
> Valentine has a circle, like Voldemort did
> Jace is a carbon copy of Draco. (Various, 2012: np)

What is interesting about this list is that nothing on it is original, even when it was in the hands of J. K. Rowling. These are all genre ideas that go a long way back: the idea of special folk who live among us who are immortal while we are doomed to live short, ordinary lives dates all the way back to fairy tales; the presumed-dead villain determined to take over the world describes Tolkien's Sauron; wizards and their secret societies were represented and feared in Renaissance literature; the magic circle is a long-standing concept in theories and mythology of necromancy; and of course the sexy bad boy à la Jace or Claire's Draco has extensive provenance in romance fiction. And I stress for all of these: *among many other* representations throughout the history of storytelling. These are all well-established and well-loved genre tropes. Mimi's chief complaint, whether she realises it or not, is that Clare writes too faithfully in the genre.

Comment threads like the one cited earlier are one of the ways that perceived misbehaviour in fandom is debated and policed. As Jamison points out 'fans can sometimes police the bounds of copyright and intellectual property (as they understand it) much more stringently than those with an actual legal stake' (2013: 234). What is notable about Clare, however, is that she has also been subject to legal action over the originality of her published work, and once again, genre is highly visible in that legal case.

On 5 February 2016, Sherrilyn Kenyon filed an action against Clare for 'trademark infringement, copyright infringement, unfair competition, false advertising, and trade dress infringement' in the Nashville division of the Tennessee District Court (Case 3:16-c-00191, cited by page numbers in what follows). Kenyon is the author of a series of adult paranormal romance novels, collectively called the *Dark-Hunter* series. The case proceeds from the grounds that Clare's Shadowhunters are an infringement of Kenyon's Dark-Hunters. According to the court documents, both series feature '[a]n elite band of warriors that must protect the world from the unseen paranormal threat . . . These hunters, whether "dark" or "shadow" preserve the balance between good and evil . . . They are both given a manual of how to conduct their mission and on how to conduct themselves when dealing with other entities and species in their fictional world' (9).

The court case has a history dating back to the first announcement of *City of Bones*' forthcoming publication. The WayBack Machine shows that the very first post at cassandraclare.com (25 May 2006) is a book blurb referring to 'the Darkhunters, [without the hyphen] a secret cadre of warriors dedicated to ridding our world of demons'. By the book's release in 2007, Clare's unhyphenated Darkhunters had become Shadowhunters, due to legal demands sent from Kenyon to Clare (4). Kenyon alleges that Clare then promised not to 'expand the use' of the term 'Shadowhunters' but that it subsequently became central to the 'complete rebranding' of Clare's work (5). Indeed, my 2015 edition has the word 'Shadowhunters' on the front cover, and in 2016, *The Mortal Instruments* television adaptation, a Netflix Original series called *Shadowhunters*, debuted. This rebranding appears to have precipitated the legal action. Kenyon's chief complaint is that the series titles are 'confusingly similar' to readerships (23) and that it was Clare's intention to 'expressly mislead and confuse the consuming public' (16). The role of Kenyon's 'consuming public', her fandom, is cited centrally in the court documents as a 'community of fans [who] immerse themselves in the detailed fictional universe contained within the world of the *Dark-Hunter* Series' (4). Indeed, Kenyon's fandom was instrumental in bringing her attention to the alleged copyright infringement: the 'PLAINTIFF was alerted by some of her distressed fans' of Clare's use of the word 'Darkhunters' in 2006 (4), and they are central to the harm she sees being done by Clare's use of 'Shadowhunters':

> The fans create their own videos, discuss the books on social media, collect memorabilia, attend conventions, dress in character inspired costumes, and are known to complain loudly about any inconsistencies they perceive within the fictional universe. (4)

This quotation from the court documents describes the fan activities and dispositions that this section has sought to elaborate: a creative and socially minded collective who are passionate about 'fictional universe[s]'. It also points to the tendency of fandom to engage in conflict – protesting about inconsistencies is familiar fan behaviour – as a specific complexion of this copyright infringement case. Kenyon suggests particular damage is done when works circulate that 'present plots and characters that are perceived as being inconsistent with the universe created in the DH Series' (22). Kenyon raises here the issue of 'canon', an ongoing obsession of fandoms. The canon of a fictional universe implies that what has already been written about settings, character, lore, and so on allows and limits subsequent possibilities within that universe. A breach of canon is a breach of a system of fictional rules, and is therefore policed by fan communities who have knowledge of and investment in those rules. The intensity of fandom, then, implicitly intensifies the harm done: this is no ordinary audience; the unimpeached integrity of the series is of particular value to them.

The perceived harm done to this invested fan community is explicitly linked in the legal documents to Kenyon's ability to earn money from the series: the 'integrity' of the series and its world and its fictional facts is 'critical to Ms. Kenyon's success and the continued commerce in her Dark-Hunter

Series' (4). Fandoms here represent 'continued commerce', or the certainty of ongoing sales. She alleges that the expansion of the Shadowhunters necessarily implies a limiting of her opportunities for 'expanding the goodwill associated with the Dark-Hunter series' (12), linking that threat to goodwill with comparative literary value: 'Consumers are less likely to read the DH series or purchase DH Series merchandise because they incorrectly associate the poor quality of DEFENDANT'S work or works with the DH series' (22). There is a sense here in which the legal battle is actually a social battle for who may claim status for their works as the authentic thing, rather than fakery, as we saw with Jace's dismissal of Madame Dorothea's books. An authentic reading experience that plays to fans, including the pleasure of consistency in a fictional fantasy setting, is at the heart of this legal action and is linked directly to Kenyon's ability to maintain and to grow her sales.

How compelling are Kenyon's claims? While Clare's original choice to call her heroes 'Darkhunters' may arouse suspicion, it is important to note that using the word 'hunters' in an urban fantasy context is a fairly generic move. Laurell K. Hamilton's *Anita Blake: Vampire Hunter* series saw first publication in 1993, predating Kenyon's novels by nearly ten years. Amazon gives us a wide range of series about Heir Hunters, Demon Hunters, Monster Hunters, Divine Hunters, Blood Hunters, and Guild Hunters; and these are only the named series. As for the similarities between the words 'dark' and 'shadow', it must be remembered that in low fantasy, words and concepts like this are indispensable: they invoke the genre strongly.

The appendix of the court papers lists pages and pages of similarities between Kenyon's work and Clare's. In many (if not most) of the examples, similarities can be explained by genre rather than by plagiarism. Humans 'cannot see through demon "glamour" (a term used by both authors)' (Appendix 2); both stories 'take place in an urban world that is not what it seems' where portals allow supernatural creatures through (Appendix 3); there is a 'sadistic' and 'charming' villain in each (Appendix 5); and a 'round chamber-hall with a magical portal entrance' (Appendix 14). All of these are generic tropes, drawn from a similar reading history. Elsewhere, Kenyon alleges '[b]oth series feature "regular humans" who are oblivious to the supernatural world' – 'Ords' in Kenyon's work and 'Mundies' in Clare's

(Appendix 2) – and yet forum poster Mimi is certain that Clare's Mundies are derived from Rowling's Muggles.

The allegations of copyright infringement were far too easily troubled on genre grounds. In February 2018, Clare addressed the court case directly on her Tumblr, providing readers with a copy of documents her lawyers had filed in response to Kenyon's, which argued for how common many of the genre tropes cited were. For example, to Kenyon's claim that 'Both Series employ a line of warriors who protect the normal world from demons', Clare's legal team has responded: 'part of long-standing literary and folkloric tradition self-evidently not originating with Kenyon'. The literary and mythological influences with which Clare frames *The Mortal Instruments* series are once again presented as a key to understanding the intentions of the text. On 31 May 2016, Kenyon dropped the copyright infringement case, leaving open only the trademark infringement case over the title 'Shadowhunters' and 'branding and packaging', which Clare is keen to point out, does not 'even slightly refer to the contents of my books' (2018: np). While adhering closely to genre conventions may be pleasurable for some readers, distasteful to others, and risky for former writers of fic, these documents show that it is highly unlikely to be legally actionable.

Conclusion

Young adult fantasy brings together two complementary social groupings: fannish fantasy audiences and youth audiences. Between them, YAF's social complexion is marked by intense investments in texts, which may lead to the formation of in-groups and out-groups. It is also marked by a higher participation by readers accustomed to orienting themselves socially in online spaces and among activities such as fan fiction. The meeting of these two types of sociality intensifies debates about genre knowledge and genre authenticity, debates that are in some ways played out both within Cassandra Clare's highly contested work itself, and in that work's relationship to other texts. Ultimately, the controversy about Clare's originality or otherwise gathers around socially contested knowledge about YAF conventions. Clare's foreword can be read as an attempt to claim dominance in this knowledge by referring to past iterations of the conventions, gesturing outside fandoms and online social battles to a long-standing Western history of literature and mythology. In so doing, she shores up her status as a real artist with inside, expert knowledge, not an outsider or pretender as she is characterised by Kenyon's lawsuit or in the many online criticisms of the originality of her work.

3 Reproducibility and Industry

From the beginning, I have been blown away by Victoria's vision for the series, which is . . . Lucas-ian – like George Lucas's vision for *Star Wars*. (HarperTeen executive editor Kirsten Pettit, in Corbett, 2016: np)

The short quotation opening this section, from a senior publishing professional involved in bringing Victoria Aveyard's YAF novel and subsequent series *Red Queen* to the market, tells a compelling story of the rise of the transmedia franchise in the genre. Pettit might have compared Aveyard's 'vision' to any number of young adult, or fantasy, or YAF literary forebears. It is significant that she reached for the name of the creator of the *Star Wars* universe: one of the most expansive and successful transmedia franchises of the late twentieth and early twenty-first centuries, and spawned from a film, not a book. Later in the same interview, Pettit speaks of encouraging Aveyard to divide her third book, which was becoming long, into two books because 'Hollywood would've done that to the third book anyway!' (in Corbett, 2016: np). This quotation likely references the film adaptations of recent YAF bestselling series *Harry Potter* and *Twilight*: in both cases, the final book in the series was split into two movies. Again, the interview reveals that Pettit was not thinking of Aveyard's work strictly as a series of books, but also as an incipient media franchise that would operate under a similar logic to other book series that had been multiply adapted across media. It is this kind of widespread transmedia activity that leads Catherine Driscoll to refer to YAF novel *Twilight* not as a book, but as a 'twenty-first-century melange of media culture' (2012: 95). In Pettit's interview, there is very little residue, if any, of an old media perspective on books. Books can be born convergent, if you will. This expectation of convergence is characteristic of twenty-first-century book culture, and driven forcefully by YAF.

There are particularly strong generic reasons for YAF's role in this drive towards transmedia reproducibility. The first reason is fandom's willingness to follow its interests in proliferative texts about fantasy worlds and lore across platforms. For Dan Hassler-Forest, the 'multidirectional prolifera-tion of transmedia world-building has ... transformed literary theory's traditional focus on the single narrative as a linear and internally coherent text' (2017: 8). The other reason is the habits of youth audiences. The Nielsen Company, best known for its BookScan book sales tracking, conducted a survey of 2,000 young adults to ascertain their influence over and interest in adaptations of YA books. The study identified several behaviours that were directly related to the expectation of adaptation, naming certain types of YA readers as 'trend ambassadors' and 'content connoisseurs' (2014: 3). The report revealed a steady growth in adaptations of YA books into movies, and showed that the list of top-selling YA authors is dominated by those whose works had been adapted to other media (4).

This section shows how YAF is powerfully placed to leverage the logics of the twenty-first-century publishing industry. Young adult audiences expect to enjoy narrative on multiple platforms, while fantasy readers are widely known to be enthusiastic and engaged fans. Young adult fiction has a legacy of seriality and a fast turnaround of new product (Nancy Drew, Sweet Valley High), where fantasy fiction has a legacy of storyworlds that live beyond their texts and create social affinities in person and online. When young adult fiction and fantasy fiction are combined in YAF, their industry and audience orientations amplify each other, disposing the texts towards storyworlds that proliferate across series and across platforms, potentially spawn franchises, and inspire widespread digital sociality (both official and unofficial). These hallmarks of the biggest success stories in contemporary publishing are related to the industry's drive towards reproducible financial success, as evidenced by its X-meets-Y sales pitches, and the audiences' need for a reproducible reading experience, as evidenced by their continued buying behaviour: as Victor Watson notes, one 'cannot read a series of twelve novels by chance' (2000: 1). This amplified orienta-tion towards reproducibility locates YAF at the centre of convergence culture in the book industry, and demonstrates how important books remain across global popular culture.

Victoria Aveyard's *Red Queen* starts with protagonist Mare Barrow living in poverty with her family in a sharply divided world of red-bloods (working class) and silver-bloods with supernatural powers (ruling class). While stealing to save her family, she unwittingly meets the king's son, Cal, who arranges for her to be employed as a servant in the palace. There, she displays an ability she did not know she had: supernatural electrokinesis. When it is discovered that a red-blood has supernatural powers, the royal family seeks to hide Mare in plain sight and thus must include her in their regular competition between the daughters of the ruling families: savage battles between young women gifted with a range of incredible destructive powers. Unlike *The Hunger Games*, Aveyard's text uses magic and supernatural powers rather than technology to drive its plot logic, aligning it more with fantasy fiction and the immensely popular superhero narrative than with science fiction, strictly speaking. Similar ideas can be found in Marie Lu's *Young Elites*, where mutant teens called malfettos seek to overthrow an oppressive government; or Leigh Bardugo's *Six of Crows*, which features gifted people, called Grisha, with a range of supernatural talents. All these texts are set in fantasy worlds that are politically and urbanly dystopian, all have fast-moving, action-based plots, and all are concerned with the exercise of special types of powers, echoing the contemporary interest in superhero battles in comics, film, and television (indeed, both Lu and Bardugo have written novelisations in the DC universe). *Red Queen*'s success has been exemplary, providing an ideal case for the study of the industrial operations of reproducibility in the genre.

The Proliferation of Storyworlds

A key attraction of fantasy fiction has always been the setting, demonstrated by the fixation of both readers and writers on the idea of 'world-building', and by the ubiquitous maps that are positioned before the narratives' first lines. But setting is not limited to the geographic or temporal location of a story: *Romeo and Juliet* is set not just in 'Fair Verona', but also within the context of a deadly feud between two families. Similarly, fantasy stories 'lay our scene' within a complex system of imagined lore, which encompasses (and is afforded and limited by) the fantasy world's history, culture, and logic. As Mark J. P. Wolf suggests, a 'wealth of details and events' may not appear in the story at all but outside it, and these 'appendices, maps, timelines, glossaries' and so on all add 'background richness' (2012: 2). *Epic Reads* features a blog post specifically about *Red Queen*'s setting, including zoomable maps, breakdowns of various areas by description, and a video interview with Aveyard about her fictional world. In this blog post, the setting is specifically linked to the plot and characters: 'The Kingdom of Norta and its surrounding lands are not only divided by war-torn borders, its people are also divided – by their blood.' Setting and lore combined make up the 'storyworld' of fantasy fiction.

Red Queen, like *Throne of Glass*, *City of Bones*, and many others, is prefaced by a map. The map acts in some ways like a prologue: it hints at action and conflict to come through geographical features and place names. Regent State, King State, and Prince State promise different aspects of plot from The Wash, The Rift, and The Choke. The difference between these place names too suggests the feudal society of the story: one set of places is associated with the ruling classes, the other with labour and hardship. The map tells us a story of haves and have-nots before the first line of prose. The fact that not all of these places appear in the text (at least not in the first book of the series) demonstrates there is a world beyond the narratable portion of the story, creating expectation and a sense of epic scope. The map defines the storyworld by suggesting that if these places are named, they must be meaningful to the story, but they also suggest that something beyond the story waits for the reader to catch up with it.

The geography of the storyworld also helps to determine its cultural dimensions. Mare Barrow, the protagonist of *Red Queen*, lives in one of the 'high, stilt buildings for which the village is named … ten feet above the muddy ground' (Aveyard, 2015: 1). Her experience of maps is to understand the places she never expects to go – 'The old classroom map swims before my eyes' (24) – even though she longs for more: '*There is so much more out there*. Beyond us, beyond the Silvers, beyond everything I know' (12). By contrast, Prince Cal has a book of 'maps, diagrams, and charts … detailing military movements from recent years and even before. Great victories, bloody defeats, weapons, and manoeuvres' (146). Cal's experience of maps is to use them as tools for power. Within and without the text, the map comes to represent the division between classes.

Just as geography helps to determine culture (muddy ground implies houses on stilts), so culture shapes geography. The Choke is so named because after 'decades of battle, the smoke of explosions is a constant fog and nothing can grow there. It's dead and grey' (16); the Ruined City is so named because '[r]adiation and fire consumed [it] once and never let it go. Now it's nothing but a black ghost ... a relic of the old world' (295). Paradoxically, Mare finds it 'comforting' to learn that maps are not necessarily geographically fixed and can alter over time (324). Her tutor, Julian, has a 'vast, colourful map pieced together from separate sheets of paper ... This is the old world, the before world, with old names and old borders we no longer have any use for' (126). Later in the text, looking at this map leads Mare to the notion that '*It's proof the world can change*' (324). In fact, the revolutionary group the Scarlet Guard, whom Mare becomes involved with, operate out of the Ruined City, which they have discovered is not radioactive at all. They call the city Naercey, 'using the old name forgotten long ago' (311). Here they have found infrastructure they can use in the revolution, including 'the Undertrain', which 'runs on the ancient tracks the Silvers never bothered to look for' (309). The impression given is that there are complex layers to the storyworld, some of which the characters may not even recognise. The more epic this complexity, the more compelling the storyworld. Hassler-Forest borrows the term 'drillable' from television studies theorist Jason Mittell to indicate a text that is both 'highly accessible to casual audiences but deliberately layered to offer rewards to "fannish" groups willing to invest more time and energy' (Hassler-Forest, 2017: 16). Aveyard builds in this drillability to *Red Queen*'s settings and its lore. In an interview on *Epic Reads*, Aveyard confesses to being a 'map geek' and tells how she began writing stories after spending time drawing maps, inspired by video game maps and historical maps. She reveals that the map of *Red Queen* is based on the north-eastern United States and, in fact, the place names are corrupted versions of existing place names. Naercey, for example, is New York City, but, as she says, 'it's hidden enough that you can't really figure it out, but once you're told you're like, "oh, of course"' (TeamEpicReads, 2015: np). In this quotation, Aveyard confirms that she offers potential extra layers to fans, as a reward for close attention to the storyworld.

The complexity of a storyworld is often hinted at rather than laid out explicitly. Farah Mendlesohn writes of fantasy fiction's impressionistic tendencies, 'constructed from *pointers*, glimpses of a world' (2008: 72). The technique of proliferation is one of the ways that fantasy texts offer glimpses, and hint at a much larger storyworld. *Red Queen* uses the history of Aveyard's storyworld to create this sense of proliferation, especially with regard to the heritage of the many noble houses and their rituals, for example, the Queenstrial when the 'daughters of the High Houses, the great Silver families, have all come to offer themselves to the prince' (Aveyard, 2015: 57). At the Queenstrial and throughout, dozens of houses are named: House Calore, House Welle, House Rhambos, House Samos, House Osanos, and so on, creating a sense that there are so many they cannot all be captured in the text. As Mare herself notes, 'I quickly lose count of them. *Just how many houses are there?* More and more join the crowd' (59). Each house is then associated with a particular supernatural power: greenies can make things grow, telkies can intercept thoughts, strongarms are physically powerful, magnetos can control metal, and so on. Learning about the history and powers of the houses frustrates Mare: 'How anyone keeps track of this, I'll never know' (132). By suggesting there is too much to keep track of, the text creates a sense that there is a vast history of houses and their superpowers that proliferates beyond sight and memory. When Mare acquires her fake heritage, in order to comply with the king's plan to keep her special ability hidden, she also acquires a long and unwieldy title, which she must hold in her head: 'Lady Mareena Titanos, born to Lady Nora Nolle Titanos and Lord Ethan Titanos, general of the Iron Legion. Heiress to House Titanos' (89). These techniques suggest parts of the world and its lore exist beyond the narratable portion of the story. In fact, 'it is precisely what does not meet the eye that gives the sense of a boundless world: there is so much to narrate that it cannot all be told' (Wilkins, 2016: 211). World-building is proliferative, creating a sense of depth, breadth, and connectedness.

But this proliferation also functions beyond individual texts: fantasy fiction is known for its proliferating narrative threads, which are not containable in single texts but generate sequels and series and related works. That is, there is an industrial element to fantasy's proliferation implied both textually and paratextually. Martens notes that texts with 'built-in world building' enable what she calls 'hypercommercialisation' (2016: 58). *Red Queen* is only the first in a series of a planned three, but now four books ('I realised there's no way I was going to get all of the story into three books,' in Corbett, 2016: np). It is common for fantasy novels to spawn series. *Red Queen*, however, is also supported by two stand-alone novellas that provide the background of the history of the conflicts in book one, including from other characters' viewpoints. To write and publish such books signals to readers that the world of *Red Queen*, like our own world, teems with innumerable places, people, happenings, and histories. Harvey calls products such as these novellas 'transmedia extensions' and suggests they foster both the understanding and the appreciation of the storyworld (2015). These extensions also contribute to what Margaret Mackey calls the 'aesthetic of the unfinish', a way in which 'our concepts of narrative and narrative conclusion are more plural and open', reshaped by the pressures of 'new technologies and new forms of capitalism' (2014: 218, 234).

Importantly, not all transmedia extensions are developed by authors and industry (Harvey, 2015: 182–3). Proliferation of fantasy storyworlds is also enthusiastically participatory. Fantasy fandoms share 'an interest in world-building as a limitless and continuously expanding narrative environment' (Hassler-Forest, 2017: 3), and enhance this proliferation through discussion, including speculation and analysis, and creative responses. Increasingly, the fannish audiences enjoying these practices are young adults, via the online social spaces they already fully inhabit. Examples online for Aveyard's storyworld include the 250-page *Red Queen* fan wiki, featuring fan-authored articles about lore and characters, as well as social discussions where readers share opinions, predictions, memes, and maps; fanfiction.net and Wattpad, which include hundreds of fan fiction stories with thousands of readers; and Tumblr, Pinterest, and DeviantArt, where hundreds of fan art images are posted. Storyworlds, then, proliferate both within and out-side of texts, inspiring avid and imaginative uptake. The combination of fan practices and young adult digital spaces amplifies storyworld proliferation and engagement. Marketers know that 'peer-to-peer marketing' is 'espe-cially effective with teens' (Martens, 2016: 60), and so young adult fan uptake is increasingly encouraged, contained, and leveraged by industry.

Henry Jenkins describes the active participation of media consumers in storyworlds as a distinct part of 'transmedia storytelling' (that is, the elaboration of storyworlds across media). Tellingly, he suggests transmedia storytelling 'demands' consumers respond in this way, suggesting that the full experience of a storyworld implies readers *necessarily* become 'hunters and gatherers, chasing down bits of the story across media channels, comparing notes with each other via online discussion groups, and collaborating to ensure that everyone who invests time and effort will come away with a richer entertainment experience' (2008: 21). Increasingly, publishers rely on this consumer behaviour to create and enrich content that keeps readers invested in storyworlds in the gaps between publications. Corbett notes that the marketing for *Red Queen* was enhanced by 'promotions that don't require the author's input', including the creation of opportunities for readers to contribute content (2016: np). One such example is the fan site where readers join the Scarlet Guard (the revolutionary band from the book). These fans are charged with sharing links across their social media in order to be rewarded with previews of content and cover art (np). This link-sharing is often pitched as 'our mission for the week', ironically reimagining working free for a large multinational corporation as revolutionary sentiment. Martens frames this as publishers using 'teens' immaterial and affective labour', which on the surface sounds quite alarming (2016: 63). Note that this is also freely given labour, and part of the economy of pleasure of fan involvement in world-building. Nevertheless, it is certainly true that publishers of YAF have become adept at capturing the social groups around storyworlds to elaborate them and to spread their reach.

Another way that reach is spread is through the deliberate generation of speculation and expectation that precedes the release of a book. Twenty-first-century convergence culture is implicated here: expectations about cross-platform, participatory, and digital culture have resulted in a cultural infrastructure where fans can be 'increasingly mobilised as essential "influencers" whose endorsement of a particular product [is] essential to . . . help attract a mass audience' (Hassler-Forest, 2017: 6). More platforms and media mean 'more information on any given topic than anyone can store in their head' and a resultant 'added incentive for us to talk among ourselves about the media we consume', which creates valuable 'buzz' (Jenkins, 2008:

4). The success of Aveyard's debut is partly due to the early buzz that was generated for it. Christina Colangelo, the marketing director who worked on *Red Queen*, suggests the buzz began with the cover reveal, five months before publication, on the world's largest YA online reader community, *Epic Reads*: 'the striking jacket got an overwhelmingly positive reaction.' This drove readers to Aveyard's social media. Aveyard's youth and 'ready-made facility' in these forums intensified the interest. HarperCollins then capitalised on that interest by reconfiguring 'all our marketing and publicity plans' to respond to 'that hunger for the book we saw in our community'. By the time it went to print, HarperTeen decided on an 'aggressive' print run of 150,000 books (in Maughan, 2015: np).

Important here is Colangelo's choice of the words 'our community'. Although it is only acknowledged on the site in small print, *Epic Reads* is wholly owned by HarperCollins, Aveyard's publisher. HarperCollins used its corporate heft to create and to populate this large and highly patronised online community, presenting reviews and information about young adult books from across all publishing houses, not just its own. However, there can be no doubt that once this audience was captured, the publisher had the potential to leverage that enthusiasm for its own ends through research and marketing, bearing out Hassler-Forest's contention that large media corporations display 'frantic and increasingly canny efforts to direct the [fan] energy that has been unleashed in directions that will maintain the existing balance of power' (2017: 17). *Red Queen* became the first debut novel ever to appear at number one on the *New York Times* YA bestseller list; within its first year, it had sold in thirty-seven foreign territories and the film rights had been acquired by Universal Studios (Maughan, 2015: np). The energy of YAF fan communities was deliberately leveraged into unprecedented publishing success.

Seriality and the Franchise

Fantasy's proliferation of storyworlds also lends itself to reproduction, shifting narrative away from closure to 'the openendedness of serialisation' (Hassler-Forest, 2017: 8). Both fantasy fiction and young adult fiction have a history of seriality (Maund, 2012: 147), although that seriality bears a different complexion for each genre.

Fantasy's series are epic and published almost painfully slowly. The fourteen books in Robert Jordan's *Wheel of Time* series were published over a twenty-three-year span (1990 to 2013), with the final three books written by Brandon Sanderson after Jordan's death in 2007. At the time of writing, readers of George R. R. Martin's *Song of Ice and Fire* series have waited eight years for the sixth book. In fact, the HBO television adaptation of the series, which presumably has vastly more complex production logistics, managed to get ahead of Martin's book in its 2017 seventh season. Young adult fiction, however, has a history replete with examples of quickly produced series. The *Sweet Valley High* series, for example, comprised more than 600 books published within twenty years (largely ghostwritten). By contrast, each book in Stephanie Meyer's *Twilight* series was published a tidy year apart.

I do not mean to suggest that YAF is the only genre that exploits the serial form. A general orientation towards series publishing is characteristic of twenty-first-century publishing 'as publishers have searched for story lines that can keep readers hooked for several books rather than just one', and these are usually genre books (Bosman, 2014: np). Editor Sean McDonald affirms readers have become 'more aware of series storytelling' and this leads to a 'sense of impatience' for readers if they feel a book series is not being published fast enough (in Bosman, 2014: np). These expectations and frustrations have in some ways been fuelled by the reconfiguration of the television industry through on-demand technology: 'the book business is upending its traditional timetable by encouraging a kind of binge reading, releasing new works by a single author at an accelerated pace' (Bosman, 2014: np). The CEO of Hachette, Michael Pietsch, speaks of this new orientation towards 'instant gratification' encouraging 'binge buying ... which encourages multibook series' (in Beckton, 2015: np).

The speed of YAF, then, becomes an asset: the publishing industry harnesses the double orientation of YAF towards reproducibility – proliferation of fantasy worlds and quick turnaround of YA books – to secure its market dominance. Always *implied* in this dominance, though, is the intense investments readers and writers may have in genres. Repeated reading behaviour – what publishers may see as repeat market behaviour – is underpinned by pleasure, and seriality can create pleasure. Victor Watson argues that the impulse to collect series fiction enhances a sense of connection to other readers, and that this 'sense of belonging' is intensified if the books also depict collective action (2000: 8). The imbricatedness of pleasurable community and convergent reproducibility is captured beautifully in this quotation from Victoria Aveyard in an interview about her *Red Queen* series:

> I'm a very indulgent writer and I always want more than a standalone, so I came into the novel knowing I wanted to write a series but I didn't know that I would get a chance to. All my favourite books and movies are franchises like *Harry Potter* and *[The] Lord of the Rings*, so that was always the dream. (in Baver, 2015: np)

Pleasure and convergence, the desires of the invested fan, and the demands of the industry are all in play in this quotation. The writer who wants to create sprawling worlds is 'indulgent', and it is a 'dream' to produce something like her 'favourite' art: this rhetoric reveals her deep attachments to her fantasy world and her genre. But note how the term 'series' slides uncritically into 'franchise', and books and their movie versions are unproblematically conflated, bringing together the economic imperatives of industry in terms of financially successful reproducibility and convergence. If world-building is the author's remit, and proliferating paratexts is the fan's, then franchising is transmedia industry's way of extending storyworlds in fantasy fiction.

Franchising describes 'ongoing, multiplied production in which parallel or successive production contexts creatively share and economically extend intellectual property resources' (Johnson, 2011: 1078). The ongoing, parallel, and successive aspects of YAF speak to the industrial aim of reproducibility, while the multiplication and extension implies its orientation towards convergence. Reproducibility and convergence are implied in the logic of YAF's seriality and franchising.

Reproducibility in the Market

Reproducibility of success is an imperative across all industries, but especially in industries where success is unpredictable such as the publishing industry. Reproducing success is easiest when it involves publishing subsequent books by an already successful author. Readers, who also want reproducibility of their reading pleasure, 'will be drawn to books by authors they have already read', and the machinery of the publishing industry – including marketers, booksellers, and publicity channels – 'will be working within established parameters: the author and his or her work is known, and hence there are obvious patterns for representing them to consumers' (Squires, 2007: 87). Mark McGurl observes, in his analysis of what he calls the 'Age of Amazon', that the novel is now 'not particularly important except as a unit of discourse in the formation of . . . a longer series' (2016: 460). But YAF has made an art of other kinds of reproducibility, not limited to seriality. Experiments in delivering 'staggered content in a quick manner' have become frequent in the field (Deahl, 2012: np). After the bestselling success of *Red Queen*, Aveyard's publisher approached Aveyard about what other notes, ideas, and histories she might have about her world and her characters. She explains: 'We didn't expect to hit the bestseller list immediately so we all started brainstorming about what else we could give fans, whether there were other stories we wanted to tell and, of course, there were' (in Corbett, 2016: np). From these notes, Aveyard developed the two novellas cited earlier, *Queen Song* and *Steel Scars*, which HarperTeen e-published, then later published in a single paperback edition as *Cruel Crown*. Her editor Kirsten Pettit notes that a 'steady stream of content between books keeps fans engaged' and 'builds excitement' for subsequent books (in Corbett, 2016: np).

Reproducibility may also take the form of the series spin-off. For example, Cassandra Clare signed with Simon & Schuster in 2012 for a 'story cycle' project called *The Bane Chronicles*. Co-authored stories were released digitally monthly, then later published in a print bind-up. The idea was to replicate an 'episodic TV show structure' (Deahl, 2012: np). This kind of spin-off, although ostensibly co-authored by Clare, extends the storyworld with other authors' labour, reminding us in some ways of the long, quickly produced teen series of the past, such as *Nancy Drew*, which was ghostwritten under the name Carolyn Keane.

But most often, publishers attempt to reproduce success generically, with different authors and storyworlds. The 'boom in sexy vampires' that followed the success of Stephanie Meyer's *Twilight* series (Levy and Mendlesohn, 2016: 201) was plainly evident to even the untrained eye: dozens if not hundreds of new titles flooded the market. These texts were marketed using what Spencer calls 'carryover', or the replication of marketing strategies from another successful text (2017: 432). Carryover ensured that the YA paranormal romance became one of the most bankable subgenres in publishing for a time, just as the YA dystopian adventure did after the success of Suzanne Collins's The Hunger Games trilogy. Of all these read-alikes, only a handful achieved anything approaching the extraordinary success of the original text; but ordinary, steady sales underpinned the market, and conventions made popular in these books continue in circulation (including in the texts discussed in this Element). As Corbett notes, '*Red Queen* shares a lot of DNA with other fantasy trilogies, many of which have struggled to find an audience in a crowded marketplace' (2016: np), while Bell writes of *Red Queen*, 'The unlikely heroine trope is on full blast. Katniss Everdeen, Tris Prior, and now Mare Barrow' (2017: np). *Red Queen* appealed to the acquiring publishers not only because it was original, but also (perhaps more so) because it was not.

In such a 'crowded marketplace', what kind of things have to happen for a book to become a success? Marketing is, of course, key in this regard. First, the size of an advance will always have a bearing on the marketing budget, as publishers seek to protect their investments (Spencer, 2017: 432). But it is not just a financial investment, but also an investment of enthusiasm within a publishing company – what Pettit calls 'in-house love' (in Corbett, 2016: np) – which may result in certain books being prioritised over others. Second, the logic of what works in marketing the major sellers can be used to market new books. If a certain jacket style or marketing strategy has worked for a comparable text, it may be reproduced, sometimes slavishly so: the covers of the *Red Queen* series each depict a bloody crown against a solid colour; the cover for Astrid Scholte's *Four Dead Queens* depicts four bloody crowns against a solid colour. Third, and probably most undeniably, much of a book's success depends on, as Aveyard notes, 'some good luck': underscoring the unpredictability of the market (in Maughan, 2015: np). While big multinationals have the resources to acquire, publish, and market potential bestsellers, bestselling success is 'serendipitous and is difficult – if not impossible – to artificially fabricate' (Martens, 2016: 58). A number of titles over the past ten years bought by publishers in reported 'significant' deals (that is, US$250,000 and above) have not generated the buzz or the sales of Aveyard, Clare, or Maas. At the date of writing this, Elly Blake's first book in the Frostblood saga has garnered just over 8,000 ratings on *Goodreads*, Kathryn Purdie's first book in the *Burning Glass* series fewer than 4,000, and Kristen Ciccarelli's first book in the *Iskara* trilogy fewer than 3,000. For comparison, Aveyard's first novel has so far attracted 329,000 ratings. There is as yet no reliable way to correlate number of *Goodreads* ratings and sales value, but the number of ratings is a fraction of the number of readers. Aveyard's book too has had a head start on the others, but the figures are still poles apart given they are the same target audience. As an aside, a small advance does not necessarily predict a small success either. It is worth noting that YA superstar John Green's first novel attracted what he calls a 'four-figure book deal', but went on to spend 141 weeks on the *New York Times* bestseller list (Maughan, 2014: np).

At the heart of the drive towards reproducibility of book success is the financial imperative of publishing. Thompson, in a Bordieusian move, tells us that publishers are interested in only two types of value, economic or symbolic (2012: 10), but the concern with sales value is increasingly urgent in a rapidly transforming marketplace. In the wake of several publishing mergers of the 1990s, Taxel showed that when multinational entertainment conglomerates acquire publishing houses, they compared their holdings in terms of profitability. A multinational may own 'television and radio stations, movie theatres, theme parks, multimedia production companies' and more (2002: 158). A novel, which might have once generated a profit of 4 per cent, may now be expected to perform in line with much more profitable entertainment commodities (160). Taxel criticises the introduction of 'fast capitalism' to the young adult publishing sector, describing it as 'the need to develop and customise new products and services quickly' (148). Taxel holds that the literary and educational value of young adult works is undermined by the change to long-standing traditions in publishing around acquisition, creation, production, and distribution (147); presumably, he is comparing this model to the twentieth-century model where gatekeeping was in the hands of librarians, teachers, and parents

(Martens, 2016: 2). Richards also identifies a 'split' between YA that is suitable for curriculum and libraries, and YA that is 'unconstrained by the regulatory concerns' of educators (2007: 153). Since Taxel made his argument, traditional publishing has contracted into even fewer hands, most recently with the merger between Penguin and Random House under the majority control of mass media behemoth Bertelsmann. Aveyard's publisher is HarperCollins, a division of Newscorp and part of Rupert Murdoch's extensive global media and broadcast holdings. There is no doubt that HarperTeen is embedded in this multinational, transmedia corporation and that reproducibility of Aveyard's newsworthy success in the publishing marketplace is its significant goal. But the influence of a transmedia environment is also felt in the possibilities afforded for maximisation of investments in creative assets through licensing subsidiary rights to other large corporations for adaptations to other media. Young adult fantasy, with its fantasy fan and digitally savvy behaviours, and its tendency towards reproducibility in franchises, is ideally suited to convergence culture.

Convergence

According to Jenkins, convergence is not simply the idea that the digital has replaced the analogue, but that old media and new media interact and flow 'across multiple media platforms' enabled by 'cooperation between multiple media and the migratory behaviour of media audiences who will go almost anywhere in search of the kinds of entertainment experiences they want' (2008: 2). In convergence culture, readers would be encouraged to 'seek out new information and make connections among dispersed media content' (3). The 'quintessential' example of this kind of 'ultra high-budget transmedia' YAF franchise is, of course, the *Harry Potter* series (Russell, 2012: 392). Here, and in other examples like it, we see not just a 'binary with 'source' on one side and 'adaptation' on the other', but 'an ongoing process through which new adaptations continually (re)develop an ever-growing metatext' (Zeller-Jacques, 2012: 143). The proliferative tendencies of YAF apply across media.

A recent survey of young adult readers found that a significant percentage now expect their books to have some kind of digital, extra-textual aspect to them (Angel, 2017: np). Such an expectation has the potential to influence which books are acquired, published, and adapted. A 'symbiotic relationship [exists] between [young adult] books and the movies: The excitement about these movies starts with the books and the fans who are engaged with the property' (Nielsen, 2014: 3). Fan behaviour around certain books makes them ripe for adaptation because readers 'want to see the characters and the worlds come to life' (3). Fans, whom Jenkins identifies partly by their attachments to the fantasy genre, have moved 'from the invisible margins of popular culture and into the centre of current thinking about media production and consumption' (2008: 12). Saler agrees, calling fans 'the most visible adherents of imaginary worlds', whose habits have become adopted by a majority in the West: 'we are all geeks now' (2012: 3). Fan tastes are a shaping influence on how books are adopted and adapted across media. There is nothing unusual about this: it is simply market forces at play. But the combined market influence of young adults and fans situates YAF right at the centre of twenty-first-century book culture's tendency towards media convergence.

Convergence spreads out across multiple platforms, working to the favour of the multinationals. For all the market influence of YAF fans, 'the relationship between producers and audiences is still a hugely asymmetrical one, and … the power of global conglomerates remains a massive obstacle for actual media democratization' (Hassler-Forest, 2017: 15). Such a sentiment underpins Taxel's earlier concerns about undue commercial influence on young adult fiction. He notes 'the continuing growth of the mass-market side of the industry, the explosive increase in the licensing and merchandising of characters from children's books and popular films, and the proliferation of a variety of series books that have assumed the status of brand names comparable to other popular commodities' and believes this works against the 'greater inclusion of long silenced, and often vilified, voices into the literary canon … a struggle that is inextricably tied to the movement for social justice and equity' (2002: 148).

Such a view suggests YA books that are overly promoted by the massive entertainment complex must necessarily be morally or ideologically weak, framing 'the branding and world building of serialised media production as franchising' in the same way that 'fast food hamburgers are understood – and maligned – as too economically rationalised and homogenously standardised to be culturally legitimate' (Johnson, 2011: 1079). Johnson suggests that we should instead understand 'franchised production and reproduction of culture as a dynamic site where power, meaning, and value collide' (1091). I am very drawn to this view as both a reader and a writer of fantasy fiction, because I still believe in the idealism of the genre. Readers have passion and purpose in their engagement with fantastic storyworlds, and while those things can absolutely be monetised by large corporations, they can never be fully owned; nor does monetisation extinguish them entirely. When we suggest that bestsellers are reducible to corporate properties, we may as well say that readers' only interactions with books come from buying them. The example cited earlier, of Keira Drake's heavily pre-promoted book being withdrawn due to fan concerns about racism, is just one example that demonstrates that the power balance between publishing conglomerate and reader does not run only one way. In fact, Hassler-Forest notes that in some cases, 'the positive revolutionary energy these highly commodified media tap into cannot be fully contained by the capitalist machinery that attempts to regulate and contain it' (2017: 19). Alexander and Black also believe that reading YAF books, especially those set in dystopic worlds, can 'provide the grounds for a new set of discourses' to 'think through systems of inequality' (2015: 233). Many of these texts (and their communities) can see the outside of global capitalism, and they critique it through their storyworlds.

Victoria Aveyard states in a reading-group guide that she was inspired by her own feelings of financial oppression about her student loan debt and the revolutionary excitement around the Occupy movement when she imagined the storyworld of *Red Queen* (2015: 389). The book ranges across a number of contemporary concerns. The manipulation of the media to the advantage of those who control it is explored in the final scenes of the book, where Queen Elara withholds vital information from the public about who killed King Tiberias. It is also Queen Elara who sets off bombs at a crowded event in order to manipulate public opinion about the Scarlet Guard, painting them as terrorists: 'Their goal is to harm innocent civilians, Silver and Red, to incite fear and hysteria' (134). Elsewhere, one of the highest houses, House Samos, is shown to be making its fortune from the war to which Red families are losing their sons and daughters: Volos Samos 'owns and operates the iron mines. Every gun in the war comes from his land' (107). But the clearest picture of class oppression in the text comes in the description of Gray Town, which is formed of a set of slums built around industrial estates: 'Beneath such a smoky sky, I doubt the workers ever see daylight. They walk between the factories and their homes, flooding the streets during a shift change' (286). These so-called techies are an oppressed working class, trapped in a cycle of poverty and work, completely foreclosed and deprived even of engagement with the natural world. The image is one of exploited second-world labour. When Mare sees them, she thinks, '*I must not forget this . . . I must not forget them*' (287).

This close first-person, present-tense narration retains urgency and directness, inviting us into Mare's world, and holding us close to her opinions. It is a technique that worked well in Collins's *The Hunger Games*, of course, and the dystopian tropes are not in any way unprecedented. But *Red Queen*, despite being thoroughly caught up in the convergent, franchised, fast-capitalist, global-corporate processes of twenty-first-century entertainment, urges us through Mare's viewpoint to hope for something better than class division and oppression. This is the power of fantasy and YA together: where reproducibility is put into service in imagining a fairer world, and those imaginings are enthusiastically read, discussed, remediated, and shared by millions of young readers, who will shape the future.

Conclusion

Young adult fantasy, then, operates industrially in ways that are extensions of the pleasures of its combined genres. Proliferation and seriality are a good fit for the twenty-first-century publishing marketplace, which is increasingly influenced by the logics of other media. Young adult fantasy has been at the heart of several blockbuster franchises, and so reproducing these successes is important to an industry characterised by the contraction of the number of publishers under large media conglomerates, and by an increasing orientation towards franchising and convergence. Industry's imperatives have found a good fit in YAF, with its insatiable, passionately active, digitally savvy readers primed to engage with new storyworlds, in whatever form or platform they might appear.

Conclusion: Creative, Cultural, Commercial

While the core business of the publishing industry remains the same – to bring books and readers together – the processes behind that core business have transformed in the twenty-first century. Young adult fantasy has been both a significant beneficiary and a significant driver of that change. At the heart of the uptake of technological advance in publishing is the concept of comparability. From acquisition, when the X-meets-Y formulation frames new texts, right through to point of sale, when Amazon informs us what 'customers who bought this item also bought', precision in positioning texts within a matrix of other, similar texts has become a chief concern of the field. Implied here is genre, the much-maligned defining concept of popular fiction, reaching a kind of apotheosis. But, as I have shown, genres are not static and neither are they handed down from on high. They are negotiated between writers, readers, and institutions, and formed and reformed across texts, social groupings, and industrial practices. This Element has sought to understand that interdependence of processes.

While genre has always been negotiated across these interrelated processes, the new publishing paradigm features more avenues than ever for those negotiations about genre to become explicit rather than implicit, conscious rather than unconscious, deliberate and targeted rather than a result of hopeful guesswork. Young adult fantasy is highly visible in popular culture due to a string of successes (some so successful the books have become household names), an enthusiastic uptake in interactive forums and creative online engagement opportunities, and a ready facility for transmedia adaptation across platforms. The combined textual, social, and industrial features associated with fantasy fiction and with young adult fiction are supercharged when they are combined. New gloss can be added to twentieth-century high fantasy tropes that have fallen out of favour with adult fantasy readers. The Chosen One, the series of trials, and the pre-modern setting are reimagined as conventions that speak to the identities and concerns of young adults. The fantasy tendency to creative elaboration and critique gains enhanced traction in online spaces. Web interoperability and global reach amplify the opinions of young readers for both vindictive and valiant reasons. Quick turnaround seriality combines with proliferative world-building to produce transmedia storyworlds that undermine traditional notions of narrative closure.

By using an expanded conceptualisation of genre, this Element has yielded a picture of YAF that goes beyond description or ideological analysis, and suggests some of the deeper creative, cultural, and commercial processes that constitute the genre: a genre that currently is perhaps the most visible, successful, and beloved way of storytelling across the world.

References

Alexander, J. and Black, R. (2015). The Darker Side of the Sorting Hat: Representations of Educational Testing in Dystopian Young Adult Fiction. *Children's Literature*, 43, 208–34.

Alkestrand, M. (2014). Righteous Rebellion in Fantasy and Science Fiction for the Young: The Example of Harry Potter. In J. Helgason, S. Kärrholm, and A. Steiner, eds., *Hype: Bestseller and Literary Culture*. Lund, Sweden: Nordic Academic Press, pp. 109–26.

Angel, K. (2017). Fluid and Adaptive Reading Requires Fluid and Adaptive Publishing. Independent Publishing Conference 2017, Melbourne, Australia, 16 November.

Attebery, B. (1992). *Strategies of Fantasy*. Bloomington: Indiana University Press.

Aveyard, V. (2015). *Red Queen*. London: Orion.

Aveyard, V. (2016). *Cruel Crown*. London: Orion.

Aveyard, V. (2016). *Glass Sword*. London: Orion.

Aveyard, V. (2017). *King's Cage*. London: Orion.

Avocado (2006). *The Cassandra Claire Plagiarism Debacle*. Available at: http://web.archive.org/web/20131022155458/http://www.journalfen.net/community/bad_penny/8985.html#intro.

Bardugo, L. (2015). *Six of Crows*. New York: Henry Holt.

Baver, K. (2015). Q & A with Victoria Aveyard. *Publishers Weekly*, 19 February. Available at: www.publishersweekly.com/pw/by-topic/childrens/childrens-authors/article/65625-q-a-with-victoria-aveyard.html.

Beckton, D. (2015). Bestselling Young Adult Fiction: Trends, Genres and Readership. *TEXT*, Special Issue 32. Available at: www.textjournal.com.au/speciss/issue32/Beckton.pdf.

Bell, A. (2017). This YA Series Is a Warning to Us All. *New York Post*, 6 February. Available at: http://nypost.com/2017/02/06/this-dystopian-fantasy-trilogy-feels-almost-too-real/.

Bell, C. (2015). Mortal Instruments' Creator Reveals How Female Authors Can Be 'Dehumanized' By Their Own Fandom. MTV.com. Available at: www.mtv.com/news/2181489/mortal-instruments-cassandra-clare-fandom/.

Berberich, C. (2015). Twentieth-Century Popular: History, Theory and Context. In C. Berberich, ed., *The Bloomsbury Introduction to Popular Fiction*. London: Bloomsbury Publishing, pp. 30–49.

Bosman, J. (2014). Impatience Has Its Reward: Books Are Rolled Out Faster. *The New York Times*, 10 February. Available at: www.nytimes.com/2014/02/11/books/impatience-has-its-reward-books-are-rolled-out-faster.html.

Botting, F. (2012). Bestselling Fiction: Machinery, Economy, Excess. In D. Glover, ed., *The Cambridge Companion to Popular Fiction*. Cambridge: Cambridge University Press, pp. 159–74.

Campbell, J. (1949). *The Hero with a Thousand Faces*. New York: Pantheon.

Cashore, K. (2008). *Graceling*. London: Gollancz.

Chowdhury, R. (2006). A Chosen Sacrifice: The Doomed Destiny of the Child Messiah in Late Twentieth-Century Children's Fantasy. *Papers: Explorations into Children's Literature*, 16(2), 107–11.

Clare, C. (2007). *City of Bones*. London: Walker Books.

Clare, C. (2008). *City of Ashes*. London: Walker Books.

Clare, C. (2009). *City of Glass*. London: Walker Books.

Clare, C. (2012). October Is Anti-Bullying Month: On Hiatuses and Hate Blogs. cassandraclare.tumblr.com. Available at: http://cassandraclare.tumblr.com/post/33442496804/october-is-anti-bullying-month-on-hiatuses-and.

Clare, C. (2018). Untitled Tumblr Entry. Available at: https://cassandraclare.tumblr.com/post/169512494064/i-heard-a-rumor-that-sherrilyn-kenyon-is-no-longer.

Clare, C. (2015). Foreword. In *The Mortal Instruments: City of Bones*. London: Walker Books, pp. i–iii.

Clute, J. (1997). Fantasy. In J. Clute and J. Grant, eds., *The Encyclopaedia of Fantasy*. Available at: http://sf-encyclopedia.uk/fe.php?nm=fantasy.

Corbett, S. (2014). How Reality Became the Hot New Thing in YA. *Publishers Weekly*, 2 May. Available at: www.publishersweekly.com/pw/by-topic /childrens/childrens-book-news/article/62116-kids-getting-real.html.

Corbett, S. (2016). Red Queen Rising: Victoria Aveyard's Expanding YA Empire. *Publishers Weekly*, 2 February. Available at: www.publishers weekly.com/pw/by-topic/childrens/childrens-authors/article/69306-red -queen-rising-victoria-aveyard-s-expanding-ya-empire.html.

Cronn-Mills, K. and Samens, J. (2010). Sorting Heroic Choices: Green and Red in the Harry Potter Septology. In D. Whitt and J. R. Perlich, eds., *Millennial Mythmaking: Essays on the Power of Science Fiction and Fantasy Literature, Films and Games*. Jefferson, NC: McFarland, pp. 5–31.

Culler, J. (1975). *Structuralist Poetics: Structuralism, Linguistics and The Study of Literature*. London: Routledge & Kegan Paul.

D'Arcens, L. (2011). Laughing in the Face of the Past: Satire and Nostalgia in Medieval Heritage Tourism. *Postmedieval*, 2(2), 155–70.

Deahl, R. (2012). Clare, S&S Team up for Shadowhunters Spinoff, in P and E. *Publishers Weekly*, 10 December. Available at: www.publishersweekly .com/pw/by-topic/childrens/childrens-book-news/article/55074-clare -s-s-team-up-for-shadowhunters-spinoff-in-p-and-e.html.

Dinshaw, C. (1999). *Getting Medieval: Sexualities and Communities, Pre- and Postmodern*. Durham, NC: Duke University Press.

Dixon, P. and Bortolussi, M. (2009). Readers' Knowledge of Popular Genre. *Discourse Processes*, 46(6), 541–71.

Driscoll, C. (2012). Girl Culture and the 'Twilight' Franchise. In A. Morey, ed., *Genre, Reception, and Adaptation in the 'Twilight' Series*. London: Routledge, pp. 95–112.

Driscoll, C. and Heatwole, A. (2017). Glass and Game: The Speculative Girl Hero. In K. Gelder, ed., *New Directions in Popular Fiction*. London: Palgrave, pp. 261–83.

Faktorovich, A. (2014). *The Formulas of Popular Fiction*. Jefferson, NC: McFarland.

Fletcher, L., Driscoll, B., and Wilkins, K. (2018). Genre Worlds and Popular Fiction: The Case of Twenty-First-Century Australian Romance. *Journal of Popular Culture*, 51(4), 997–1015.

Fradenburg, L. (1997). 'So that we may speak of them': Enjoying the Middle Ages. *New Literary History*, 28(2), 205–30.

Frow, J. (2007). 'Reproducibles, Rubrics, and Everything You Need': Genre Theory Today. *PMLA*, 122(5), 1626–34.

Green, P. (2016). Cassandra Clare Created a Fantasy Realm and Aims to Maintain Her Rule. *The New York Times*. online, 23 April. Available at: www.nytimes.com/2016/04/24/fashion/cassandra-clare-shadowhunters-lady-midnight.html.

Harvey, C. B. (2015). *Fantastic Transmedia*. London: Palgrave Macmillan UK.

Hassler-Forest, D. (2017). *Science Fiction, Fantasy, and Politics: Transmedia World-Building beyond Capitalism*. London: Rowman and Littlefield.

Hills, M. (2002). *Fan Cultures*. London: Routledge.

Jamison, A. (2013). *Fic: Why Fanfiction Is Taking Over the World*. Dallas, TX: BenBella Books.

Jauss, H. R. (1970). Literary History as a Challenge to Literary Theory. *New Literary History*, 2(1), 7–37.

Jauss, H. R. (1982). *Toward an Aesthetic of Reception*. Translated by T. Bahti. Minneapolis: University of Minnesota Press.

Jenkins, H. (2008). *Convergence Culture: Where Old and New Media Collide*. New York: New York University Press.

Jenkins, H. (2014). Textual Poachers. In K. Hellekson and K. Busse, eds., *The Fan Fiction Studies Reader*. Iowa City: University of Iowa Press, pp. 26–43.

Johnson, D. (2011). Devaluing and Revaluing Seriality: The Gendered Discourses of Media Franchising. *Media, Culture & Society*, 33(7), 1077–93.

Jones, B. (2014). Fifty Shades of Exploitation: Fan Labor and Fifty Shades of Grey. *Transformative Works and Cultures*, 15.

Jones, W. E. (2014). Katniss and Her Boys: Male Readers, the Love Triangle and Identity Formation. In D. A. E. Garriott, W. E. Jones, and J. Tyler, eds., *Space and Place in The Hunger Games: New Readings of the Novels*. Jefferson, NC: McFarland, pp. 60–82.

Kaplan, J. (2011). Why Literacy (and Young Adult Literature) Matters: A Review of Current Research. *The ALAN Review*, Summer, 69–72.

Kenyon v. *Clare* (2016). US District Court, Middle District of Tennessee. Exhibit 3 to Complaint. Dark-Hunter / Shadowhunter Comparison. Available at: www.courtneymilan.com/cc-complaint/1–3.pdf.

Levy, M. and Mendlesohn, F. (2016). *Children's Fantasy Literature: An Introduction*. Cambridge: Cambridge University Press.

Listopia. YA Fiction Featuring Fangirls, Fanboys, or General Fandom (no date). Available at: www.goodreads.com/list/show/84884.YA_Fiction_Featuring_Fangirls_Fanboys_or_General_Fandom.

Lu, M. (2014). *The Young Elites*. London: Penguin Random House.

Maas, S. J. (2012). *Throne of Glass*. London: Bloomsbury.

Maas, S. J. (2013). *Crown of Midnight*. London: Bloomsbury.

Maas, S. J. (2014). *Heir of Fire*. London: Bloomsbury.

Mackey, M. (2014). Roy and the Wimp: The Nature of an Aesthetic of Unfinish. In M. Reimer, N. Ali, D. England and M. D. Unrau, eds., *Seriality and Texts for Young People*. London: Palgrave Macmillan, pp. 218–36.

Marten, M. (2016). *Publishers, Readers, and Digital Engagement*. London: Palgrave Macmillan.

Maughan, S. (2014). John Green Celebrates 10 Years of 'Looking for Alaska'. *Publishers Weekly*, 18 December. Available at: www.publishersweekly.com/pw/by-topic/childrens/childrens-authors/article/65089-john-green-celebrates-10-years-of-looking-for-alaska.html.

Maughan, S. (2015). 'Red Queen': A Bestseller Is Crowned. *Publishers Weekly*, 26 February. Available at: www.publishersweekly.com/pw/by-topic/childrens/childrens-book-news/article/65716-red-queen-a-bestseller-is-crowned.html.

Maund, K. (2012). Reading the Fantasy Series. In E. James and F. Mendlesohn, eds., *The Cambridge Companion to Fantasy Literature*. Cambridge: Cambridge University Press, pp. 147–53.

McGurl, M. (2016). Everything and Less: Fiction in the Age of Amazon. *Modern Language Quarterly*, 77(3), 447–71.

McHale, B. (2010). Genre Fiction. In D. Herman, J. Manfred, and M. Ryan, eds., *Routledge Encyclopaedia of Narrative Theory*. Digital edition.

Mendlesohn, F. (2001). Crowning the King: Harry Potter and the Construction of Authority. *Journal of the Fantastic in the Arts*, 12(3), 287–308.

Mendlesohn, F. (2008). *Rhetorics of Fantasy*. Middletown, CT: Wesleyan University Press.

Meyer, S. (2005). *Twilight*. London: Atom.

Miller, L. (2016). The Shadowhunters vs. the Dark-Hunters. *Slate*. 17 February. Available at: www.slate.com/articles/arts/culturebox/2016/02/author_sherrilyn_kenyon_sues_cassandra_clare_for_copyright_infringement.html.

Milliot, J. (2015). The Hottest (and Coldest) Book Categories of 2014. *Publishers Weekly*, 19 February.

Milliot, J. (2016). The Hot and Cold Book Categories of 2015. *Publishers Weekly*, 14 January.

Milliot, J. (2017). Adult Nonfiction Stayed Hot in 2016. *Publishers Weekly*, 13 January.

Mittell, J. (2004). *Genre and Television: From Cop Shows to Cartoons in American Culture*. New York: Routledge.

Neale, S. (1995). Questions of Genre. In B. K. Grant, ed., *Film Genre Reader II*. Austin: University of Texas Press, pp. 159–83.

Nielsen. (2014). *Young Adult Adaptation Fanship: Understanding and Engaging Fans*. Available at: www.nielsen.com/us/en/insights/reports/2014/young-adult-adaptation-fanship.html.

Palumbo, D. E. (2005). The Monomyth in Gene Wolfe's The Book of the New Sun. *Extrapolation*, 46(2), 189–234.

Pandemonium Club (no date). Available at: http://pandemoniumclub.livejournal.com/.

Phillips, L. (2015). Real Women Aren't Shiny (or Plastic): The Adolescent Female Body in YA Fantasy. *Girlhood Studies*, 8(3), 40–55.

Prensky, M. (2001). Digital Natives, Digital Immigrants Part 1. On the Horizon. *On the Horizon*, 9(5), 1–6.

Richards, C. (2007). Addressing 'Young Adults'? The Case of Francesca Lia Block. In N. Matthews and N. Moody, eds., *Judging a Book by Its Cover: Fans, Publishers, Designers, and the Marketing of Fiction*. Aldershot: Ashgate, pp. 147–60.

Roth, J. and Flegel, M. (2013). 'I'm not a lawyer but . . . ': Fan Disclaimers and Claims against Copyright Law. *Journal of Fandom Studies*, 1(2), 201–18.

Russell, J. (2012). Authorship, Commerce, and Harry Potter. In D. Cartmell, ed., *A Companion to Literature, Film, and Adaptation*. London: Blackwell, pp. 391–407.

Saler, M. (2012). *As If: Modern Enchantment and the Literary Prehistory of Virtual Reality*. Oxford: Oxford University Press.

Scalzi, J. (2006). *Crimes of Fanfic, Whatever*. Available at: www.scalzi.com/whatever/004392.html.

Schwabach, A. (2009). The Harry Potter Lexicon and the World of Fandom: Fan Fiction, Outsider Works, and Copyright. *University of Pittsburgh Law Review*, 70, 387–423.

Spencer, K. (2017). Marketing and Sales in the US Young Adult Fiction Market. *New Writing*, 14(3), 429–43.

Squires, C. (2007). *Marketing Literature: The Making of Contemporary Literature in Britain*. Houndmills: Palgrave Macmillan.

Steiner, A. (2015). Introduction. In J. Helgason, S. Kärrholm, and A. Steiner, eds., *Hype: Bestsellers and Literary Culture*. Lund, Sweden: Nordic Academic Press, pp. 7–40.

Steveker, L. (2015). Alternative Worlds: Popular Fiction (Not Only) for Children. In C. Berberich, ed., *The Bloomsbury Introduction to Popular Fiction*. London: Bloomsbury Publishing, pp. 147–62.

Stiefvater, M. (2012). *The Raven Boys*. New York: Scholastic.

Taxel, J. (2002). Children's Literature at the Turn of the Century: 'Toward a Political Economy of the Publishing Industry'. *Research in the Teaching of English*, 37(2), 145–97.

Taylor, L. (2011). *Daughter of Smoke and Bone*. London: Hodder and Stoughton.

TeamEpicReads (2015). A Guide to Red Queen's Kingdom of Norta. *Epic Reads*. Available at: www.epicreads.com/blog/a-guide-to-red-queens-kingdom-of-norta/.

Thompson, J. B. (2012). *Merchants of Culture: The Publishing Business in the Twenty-First Century*. John Wiley & Sons.

Todorov, T. (1973). *The Fantastic: A Structural Approach to a Literary Genre*. Translated by R. Howard. Cleveland, OH: Case Western Reserve University Press.

Todorov, T. (1977). An Introduction to Verisimilitude. In *The Poetics of Prose*. Translated by R. Howard. Oxford: Basil Blackwell, 80–8.

Tolmie, J. (2006). Medievalism and the Fantasy Heroine. *Journal of Gender Studies*, 15(2), 145–58.

Trigg, S. (2008). Medievalism and Convergence Culture: Researching the Middle Ages for Fiction and Film. *Parergon*, 25(2), 99–118.

tvtropes. Just for Fun/X Meets Y. *tvtropes*. Available at: https://tvtropes.org/pmwiki/pmwiki.php/JustForFun/XMeetsY.

tvtropes. The Chosen One. *tvtropes*. Available at: https://tvtropes.org/pmwiki/pmwiki.php/Main/TheChosenOne.

Various (2012). If You've Read Mortal Instruments You'll Find This Interesting. *Harry Potter and the Deathly Hallows Discussion*. In *Goodreads* [Online]. Available at: www.goodreads.com/topic/show/1007293-if-you-ve-read-mortal-instruments-you-ll-find-this-interesting.

Verboord, M. (2011). Cultural Products Go Online: Comparing the Internet and Print Media on Distributions of Gender, Genre and Commercial Success. *Communications*, 36(4), 441–62.

Watson, V. (2000). *Reading Series Fiction: From Arthur Ransome to Gene Kemp*. London: Routledge.

Wilkins, K. (2005). The Process of Genre: Authors, Readers, Institutions. *Text*, 9(2). Available at: www.textjournal.com.au/oct05/wilkins.htm.

Wilkins, K. (2016). From Middle Earth to Westeros: Medievalism, Proliferation and Paratextuality. In K. Gelder, ed., *New Directions in Popular Fiction*. London: Palgrave Macmillan.

Wolf, M. J. P. (2012). *Building Imaginary Worlds: The Theory and History of Subcreation*. New York: Routledge.

Wright, D. (2015). *Understanding Cultural Taste: Sensation, Skill and Sensibility*. London: Palgrave Macmillan.

Yang, T. (2016). How Female Superheroes and Posting Stories Online Changed Sarah J. Maas's Life. *Philippine Daily Inquirer*, 8 April.

Available at: http://lifestyle.inquirer.net/226359/how-female-superheroes-and-posting-stories-online-changed-sarah-j-maas-life/

Zeller-Jacques, M. (2012). Adapting the X-Men: Comic-Book Narratives in Film Franchises. In D. Cartmell, ed., *A Companion to Literature*, *Film*, *and Adaptation*. London: Blackwell, pp. 143–58.

Cambridge Elements

Publishing and Book Culture

SERIES EDITOR
Samantha Rayner
University College London

Samantha Rayner is a Reader in UCL's Department of Information Studies. She is also Director of UCL's Centre for Publishing, co-Director of the BloomsburyCHAPTER (Communication History, Authorship, Publishing, Textual Editing and Reading) and co-editor of the Academic Book of the Future BOOC (Book as Open Online Content) with UCL Press.

ASSOCIATE EDITOR
Rebecca Lyons
University of Bristol

Rebecca Lyons is a Teaching Fellow at the University of Bristol. She is also co-editor of the experimental BOOC (Book as Open Online Content) at UCL Press. She teaches and researches book and reading history, particularly female owners and readers of Arthurian literature in fifteenth- and sixteenth-century England, and also has research interests in digital academic publishing.

ABOUT THE SERIES

This series aims to fill the demand for easily accessible, quality texts available for teaching and research in the diverse and dynamic fields of Publishing and Book Culture. Rigorously researched and peer-reviewed Elements will be published under themes, or 'Gatherings'. These Elements should be the first check point for researchers or students working on that area of publishing and book trade history and practice: we hope that, situated so logically at Cambridge University Press, where academic publishing in the United Kingdom began, it will develop to create an unrivalled space where these histories and practices can be investigated and preserved.

Cambridge Elements

Publishing and Book Culture
Young Adult Publishing

Gathering Editor: Melanie Ramdarshan Bold
Melanie Ramdarshan Bold is Associate Professor at University College
London. Her main research interest centres on contemporary authorship,
publishing, and reading, with a focus on books for children and young
adults. She is the author of *Inclusive Young Adult Fiction: Authors of Colour in
the United Kingdom* (2018).

ELEMENTS IN THE GATHERING

A full series listing is available at: www.cambridge.org/epbc

Printed in the United States
By Bookmasters